BERT HEL

Topics of Business Consultancy

From the series: Orders of Success

Hellinger
PUBLICATIONS

10 9 8 7 6 5 4 3 2 1
2013 2012 2011 2010

Published by

Hellinger PUBLICATIONS

Sonnleitstr. 37
83404 Bischofswiesen • Germany
Postfach 2120
83462 Berchtesgaden
www.Hellinger .com

Cover / Satz & Gestaltung:
Paper@Screen
Anna W. Moderegger
www.paperscreen.tv

Druck & Bindung:
Kösel, Altusried – Krugzell

ISBN 978 -3-00-029320-7

Translated by
Angelika Schenk
Revised an edited by
Suzi Tucker

Porträt: Riccardo Desiderio
ww.riccardodesiderio.com

Bert Hellinger

Topics of Business Consultancy

From the series: Orders of Success

Hellinger
PUBLICATIONS

CONTENT

CONTENT

Introduction

This third volume in the series I published as 'Orders of Success' turns to a range of topics that may play a decisive role in either success or failure in many enterprises, because their implication are either not known, or knowingly ignored.

Every one of these topics has to do with one's own family. Either with one's family of origin or with one's present family, in the most comprehensive sense. For it also includes former and parallel relationships.

The orders of success reveal themselves as orders of love in many ways, as the orders of an inclusive love, that concedes belonging to all people who belong now or did belong earlier, giving them their appropriate place and the rights they have accordingly.

This book also goes beyond the narrow frame of a business consultancy primarily oriented to the concrete facts. This consultancy includes our whole life, and it acknowledges that our enterprises and professions remain embedded in the larger events in our life, serving as well as obeying their requirements.

So this book also serves beyond the factual consultancy in profession and enterprise, it serves as a guide for our life, in the widest sense.

The practical examples in this book were chosen from the courses I recently offered in various countries, on the subject '*Laws of success in business and in profession*'. The variety of issues covered here makes it possible to follow up on this subject in different contexts. Then you may transfer the insights all the more easily to your personal situation, to your own profession and your own enterprise, to your own life.

Like its predecessors in this series 'Orders of success', this book is at the same time a book of wisdom. It takes us into depths, where we know ourselves at home differently, connected in different ways, and with a different sense of freedom.

Many insights that you might find shocking in the beginning, reveal themselves as comforting a little later. They serve another love, an encompassing love. They reconcile and unite what was separated for a long time, and they lead to another success, a wider and deeper and richer success. And the same goes for happiness.

Bert Hellinger

The background

How does it all come to light, how do we get to see these hidden connections and their importance for our success or failure?

Through the help of family-constellations in their new advanced form. What this means in specific situations, and how I proceed, you will see in the different examples I will describe in detail. And afterwards I will give explanations. This way you can join in and re-enact the decisive steps in your mind, as they apply to your personal situation.

To help you form an image of the process, I'll briefly explain the procedure. For instance, two representatives are arbitrarily chosen from the present group. One of them, usually a woman, will represent the enterprise or the profession, the second one will represent the entrepreneur or the person with this profession or task. The representatives have no or very little information about the enterprise or the profession or the person who has a constellation.

After a while the representatives are taken by a movement that comes neither from their ideas nor from their personal intention. Moved as if by magic, they move in a way as if acting out a drama in front of the participants and the person whose constellation it is. Something hidden comes to light. In a very short time, the constellation reveals what it is all about in its depth. At the same time, it points towards a solution that is due, if success is to be safeguarded and failure to be averted.

For instance, a representative for the profession or the enterprise is looking to the ground. She even kneels down as if she wants go to a dead person lying there. The representative for the person whose constellation it is, is also drawn to the ground, to go to someone who appears to be lying there.

Who the dead person is, need not to said. Secrets are not dragged into the light here. Yet it is clear that someone is missing, someone who does not have their right place in the family of the person whose constellation it is.

I don't need to go any further with this here. The examples in this book explain these things and deepen your understanding. Here I just wanted to show you that in reading this book you venture out on many experiences, adventures of life in its fullness, and towards more life, instead of less.

Re-orientation in the flow of time

Concerning time, we differentiate between past, present, and future. According to this image, time flows from our past through our presence, and from there, into our future. So coming from some past it flows beyond what was before, moving to the now, and from the now it to it is on the way what will be later. This means: time has left the past behind, it is here now, and it moves on to what is coming.

This is a linear image of time. According to this image, we look backwards as well as forwards. In the present we look behind us, as well as ahead.

Our life and our enterprises have already been here with us for some time. We can move within them because they are already there. So we move in their present and at the same time, in their past. The past lives on in them in the moment. It is still there in them, and quite alive. In the river of time it is by no means lost. The past is the foundation on which the present can be built. In a more biological image, we could say, the past is the root from which the present feeds.

When the past in its function as the foundation starts to get cracks, the house that was built on it begins to crumble. After a while it will collapse. When a tree's taproot begins to rot, it will eventually fall over, and with it, its future. There will be no fruit, no seeds. Then the tree itself is also gone.

Where do we look when we look at our enterprise and at the success we expect from it? First of all we look at the foundations so we know to what extent it will be able to carry its building. Will they be strong enough in the long run? Or in the other image, we have a look at the tap root. Is it still intact, to draw water from the depth, and the other roots, can they also stabilize and feed the tree, and thereby support the tree to live and to grow and to bear fruit? And we may have to be realistic and check out if there is too much damage in the foundation to uphold the house for much longer, or too much decay in the tree's root system to keep it alive.

In a family constellation it comes to light, how strong the foundations of an enterprise are, how sturdy the roots are, to keep it going. Therefore out first focus must be on something that went wrong in the past, that fell into disarray. When it comes to light, it will show if it can be repaired, returned to order, and also, if the entrepreneur is capable and willing to do so. Whether the entrepreneur has still got some time left to attend to this, or if it's too late.

It will also show whether there are new options in sight, for a new enterprise for instance, perhaps even with new employees and a new project. Here, our focus can be directed into the future. The past is allowed to be in the past, and we are free from old burdens.

The question is, can entrepreneurs who are in this situation, release themselves form the past internally, so that they can truly let it be over, so that they are no longer burdened by the past, and therefore, able to re-orientate themselves with full attention towards the next project ahead.

What happens to the future then? It is already having its effect on the present, it is already beginning to fill it.

So where does time flow then? Is it past, future, and present at once? Can we let it be over in the present, and really let the coming time become real in the present?

In one sense, we are delivered to time. But in another way, we largely have it in our hands.

So where does time flow, or run? Primarily, in ourselves. It serves us, when we take it, as it is given to us, past, present, and coming. It sets us limitations when we allow it to set us limitations. It lifts us over old limitations, when we look forward together with it, with time fully behind us, successfully backing us.

First Topic

Our success and our mother

Introductory remarks
Purity of heart

Purity of heart is in the spirit. It begins in the spirit, in a pure spirit.

Our spirit becomes pure through its direction. The movements of the pure spirit and the pure heart are directed towards what is coming. The pure heart leaves everything from the past behind, it becomes pure of all past.

What happens with what is past? It becomes pure as well, purely past, completely past. For the pure heart, the past does not attach to anything any more, neither within itself, nor anywhere else. In the pure heart, the past is allowed to be pure, and the past does become pure through the pure heart.

Our mother, for instance, becomes pure through our pure heart, pure from our memories that dim her pure image. The pure heart succeeds in this purity through a pure spirit. The pure spirit sees mother as pure in the service of life, pure in the service of our life that reached us purely, through her, perfectly pure.

So our pure heart is kindly turned to her with a pure love, devoid of all memory from the past. This love is attentive to the here and now, attentive to what happens with love in this moment, attentive to what flows with love from this pure heart now, attentive to this love, empty of everything from the past. Resting in a pure movement to mother, it is open in wonderment. What will this love bring about in its pure creativity, what new things will arise from it now?

So where does our heart's purity begin? It begins in our spirit, in a pure spirit. In our relationship with our mother we come into harmony with the creative spirit that brought all things into life, and still creates everything now- as it is. And we hear the spirit say: "See, I make all things new."

Example: Now I am rich

From a course about the laws of success in São Paulo • 31.3. – 1.4. 2009

Hellinger *to a man:* What is your issue?

Man: I have three activities. I work in agriculture. I inherited the agricultural businesses from my father. These businesses have not been doing well for twenty years.

My second activity is: I have a commercial business. I import diagnostic products for medical purposes.

The third branch is an industry. We manufacture products for diagnostic purposes.

Hellinger: You have a lot to do. What is the problem?

Man: The work in the agricultural production has been doing poorly for the 20 years, and the other two branches have been going badly for three years.

Hellinger: What does bad mean?
Man *with a deep sigh: There are financial difficulties, and poor results. The businesses don't grow any more.*

Hellinger: That was a heavy sigh.
Man: There are also other problems apart from the issues of finances and growth. It is a family problem. I have two children, an older boy, and a girl, a younger one. The older one used to work with me. That did not go well, and ten years ago he left the business. Then my daughter came into the business. She brought her husband along, my son in law. I feel really bad about it. My son feels pushed out of the family, und the siblings don't get along with each other..

Hellinger: What shall we do there?
Man: I would love to know what we shall do there.

Hellinger places the man, and opposite him, a representative for his mother. The man sighs deeply, he closes his eyes in between, but he does not move. The mother puts both her hands on her chest. The man wipes away some tears. Then he takes a small step towards her. The mother smiles at him.

Slowly, after several small steps, frequently wiping the tears from his face, he reaches her. He stretches his hand out for her and then also takes her other hand. The mother strokes his face and puts her hand on his chest

Hellinger: Say to her: "Dear Mama."
Man: Dear Mama.

Hellinger: "Thank you."
Man: Thank you.

Hellinger: "Now I am rich."
Man: Now I am rich.

The mother draws him closer. He puts his head on her shoulder. She strokes his head. The man cries. After a while both take some steps backwards.

Hellinger chooses three women to represent his three businesses. He places them side by side in front of the man. The man has his arms folded behind his back.

The first business has its arms folded in front of the chest. The second business opens its arms wide, but the man goes to the third one. Both put one arm around each other.

Hellinger *to the man:* Was this a good choice? Which one of the businesses is the strongest?

He points with his hand to the first one.

Hellinger: Go back once more. Which of the three businesses is the strongest?

As he wants to ask: You can see it, you just have to look.
The man goes to the first business and strokes its back with one hand.

Hellinger *to the first business:* How are you with him?
First Business: I sense a burden. I am not well. Something makes me feel uncomfortable.
Hellinger *to the third business:* How was it for you with him?
Third business: *Okay, but better without him.*

Laughing in the group

Hellinger: Strange, how blind one can be. We all see it. It's only him who can't see it.

The man paces restlessly up and down. The first business is drawn to the ground.

Hellinger: There's only one left that I can ask.
To the mother: How are you?
Mother: *I am sad.*

The second business leans with its back on the mother.

Hellinger *to the representatives:* Thank you all.
To the Man: Come and sit with me again. How are you now?
Man: I am confused.

Hellinger: What have you done to your mother?
Man: I think I did not like her enough.

Hellinger: There is more. From what I could see, I have the image you caused her harm..
To the group: It is quite clear. He can't see the greatness. He could not see the greatness of this one business, even though it was plain to see. This is what you get when you can't see the greatness of your mother!
Man: I think, my father forced me, to really look out for my mother and to care for her for the rest of my life, once he had passed away.

Hellinger *after a while:* This is condescending.
Man *nods:* That's one of my mistakes, arrogance.

He laughs as he says it.

Hellinger: You don't get away that lightly with me.
A mistake? You have offended a law of life.

He nods.

Hellinger *to the group:* It's not as if he' bad, But it is a violation of a law of life. Those who violate this law, fail.

He nods.

Hellinger: Is your mother still alive?
Man: She is 93 and has Alzheimer's.

Hellinger: Who cares for her?
Man: I do.

Hellinger: That's beautiful, very beautiful. Close your eyes. Tell her: "I serve."
Man: I serve.

Hellinger: "With love."
Man: With love.

Hellinger after a while: Now I am the little one.
Man: Now I am the little one.

He lowers his head, breathes deeply and cries, sighs deeply, and opens his eyes.

Hellinger calls the representative for the second business back to the stage and places the man opposite her once more.

HELLINGER *to the man:* You say to her: "I serve."
MAN: I serve.

HELLINGER: Say it from the heart, like you said it to your mother.

He goes towards her, but she backs away from him.

HELLINGER: She moves away from you. You can't go there so assertively, as if you were the big one. Go back once more.
Tell her: "Here I am the little one."
MAN: Here I am the little one.

HELLINGER: "I serve."
MAN: I serve.

HELLINGER: "With you I serve life."
MAN: With you I serve life.

HELLINGER: "Like my mother served me."
MAN: Like my mother served me.

He goes towards her very slowly and reaches one hand out to her. She has both arms spread out, but as he comes too close, she hesitates.

HELLINGER: Go back two steps once more.
Tell her: "You are the great one here."

Man: You are the great one here.

Hellinger: "You lead."
Man: You lead.

Hellinger: "I serve."
Man: I serve.

Hellinger: "Many."
Man: Many.

Hellinger: "With you."
Man: With you.

The business nods and moves the whole body.

Hellinger to the business: Tell him: "Hold me."
The Business: Hold me.

The man goes towards the business, and the two embrace warmly. The business wants to sink to the ground, but he holds it firmly. In his arms it looks limp.

Hellinger asks the mother's representative to stand behind the business. Slowly the business straightens up again.

Hellinger: Tell your mother: "I serve in memory of you."
Man: I serve in memory of you.

The mother goes close to the business. Over the business, the man reaches out his hand to the mother. The business straightens up and embraces him. He is still crying and holding his mother's hand. The mother strokes his head and his arm. Then she slowly withdraws. The man goes towards her with the business. The three of them embrace.

HELLINGER: Success has the face of the mother.
To the man, once he sits next to him again: How are you now?
MAN *laughs: Better and weaker.*

HELLINGER: Not weaker, just smaller.

The man nods.

HELLINGER: Now there's only one thing left to do now. Look at me. Get into it!

He laughs loudly and gives Hellinger a pat on the thighs.

HELLINGER: All the best to you.

More examples about this topic you'll find under:

Inheritance

Double displacement:

Second topic

Where have all the children gone?

Introductory remarks

Where have they gone? Where are we going?

Where have all the children gone? Where are they, the still born, those who died young, the miscarried ones, the aborted ones, the disowned ones, those who were given away? They are all gone and yet still here.

Where are they? They are there, for instance in our businesses, quite in the background, hidden and powerful. In our businesses they sometimes rise again and make themselves felt and known, until such time that we take them into our heart. May be just for a little while, but with love.

They are away from us, and at the same time they have arrived elsewhere. Especially those who are already dead, often for a long time already.

Why do they make themselves felt in our lives? Do they need something? Can we and must we do something for them? Do we need something from them? Do they bring themselves to our attention, because they want to give us something and serve us?

Is it perhaps, that they are taken by the hand by other powers? So when they want to get our attention, is it that they want to make us aware of these powers and guide us back to them? Is it more us, who need them, for our completeness?

As we miss them, so we miss our success later in life, and so we miss our completeness.

The question is: How do they come back to us? How does our success come back to us? Or posing the question the other way round: How do we get back to that love that includes all who belonged to us? How do we arrive, where we already are?

We arrive in consonance with that creative power who guides every fate. It guides these children's fate, it guides their parents' fate, it guides the fate of our successes and our failures. It guides every fate individually and also together with everyone else. Sometimes it takes us to painful detours, to bring us back to our senses.

How do we come into consonance with this creative power, with this creative power, that recreates everything anew at any moment, and holds everything in its being?

Casting our eyes on what is ahead of us, in the service of life.

In this forward movement, what do we leave behind? What do we take along in this forward movement?

We leave our feelings of guilt behind, our feeling of guilt, that blames us and others. What are we trying to achieve with every feeling of guilt, and especially with every attempt of doing penance, to atone for some guilt, hoping to get rid of it that way, by paying for it? It is an attempt to take our fate into our own hands, and this attempt turns it around in a way that is taking life instead of giving life. Guilt and atonement oppose life, instead of serving life, saying yes to our life, and successfully serving others with our life.

How can we succeed in this?

We gather all the people who belonged to us and still belong to us, and we take them along into the future with us. Maybe it is the other way round. We let them guide us. We follow them, so that they take us along with them into this future, so that they take us along successfully. Purified, as a blessing for many, we let them take us along into the full life, in this movement of reunion and renewed oneness.

Example: *Autistic child*

From the course on the laws of success in Hong Kong • 14. – 16. June 2009

Hellinger *to a man:* What is it about?
Man: I have a choice between several enterprises. I am a bit frustrated in this. I had two enterprises, but I separated from one of them.

Hellinger: What kind of enterprises are they?
Man: One is run by several family members.

Hellinger: What kind of business?
Man: It's about building material. I work with my wife's family.

Hellinger: Where did this business come from?

MAN: From my wife's brother. He started it and has been running it for 10 years.

HELLINGER: Is your wife a partner in this business?
MAN: Yes.
HELLINGER *to the group:* To begin with, I'll demonstrate the dynamics in this business.

Hellinger chooses a representative for this business. He places the business opposite the representative of the wife's brother, four meters apart. To the left of the wife's brother, he places a representative for the man's wife, and to her left he places the man himself.

The business withdraws far away. Hellinger asks the man and his wife to turn away from the business. The he chooses a female representative for the money that was needed to start the business, and places her with the others.

The money is quite restless. Hellinger places a man opposite the money. The man himself takes his wife's representative in his arms and strokes her head.

The money folds its arms in front of its chest. The man's wife's brother stands next to the added man, and with him, he walks slowly to the business.

Hellinger places the business in front of the money. The money has turned away. It holds its arms folded in front of its chest, as if it was in a lot of pain. Then it kneels down and looks to the ground.

Hellinger asks a man to lie in front of the money, with his back on the ground. The money takes the man's hand.

Hellinger *to the group:* What can we see here? The business withdraws, it doesn't want to belong to anyone. The money feels drawn to a dead person. It came from a dead person. Therefore the business cannot invest the money for itself.

To the business: How are you now?

The Representative of the Business: I am angry. When I stood in front of the money, I got upset with it. My hands are cold.

Hellinger *to the group:* From the movements here we can see: This business cannot survive.

To the representatives: You can sit down.

Hellinger *to the man:* Your first question was, if this business can survive. We could see, this business cannot succeed, whatever the reasons might have been. We don't need to know these reasons. It was a good decision to turn your back on this business. Is your wife still connected to it?

Man: My wife left this business long before me, seven years ago.

Hellinger: That was a good decision. We can leave this question. The next question concerned a new enterprise. Do you want to start a new enterprise?

Man: Yes.

Hellinger: How many options do you have?

Man: Three

Hellinger: Can you list them?
Man: The first one continues on with the former one. On this base I could start a new business.

Hellinger: What kind of business is it?
Man: A business for building materials.

A second business is a mine, the third one is an enterprise that my wife founded. It is a Non Profit Organization.

Hellinger: Is that a business at all? If yes, it would be her business, not yours.
Man: Seven years ago I persuaded my wife to leave the former busines , and to start an organization of her own. I am the president of this organization. This organization helps autistic children.

Hellinger *to the group:* We'll have a look at it.

Hellinger chooses female representatives, one for the business for building materials, and one for the mine. They stand next to each other, four meters apart. Opposite them also four meters apart, he places the man and a representative for his wife. The mine turns away.

Hellinger chooses a man as a representative for an autistic child, and he places this man opposite the man, 4 meters away.

The autistic child gets on his knees and slithers over to the man. The man goes towards it, kneels down with him and embraces it lovingly, wiping his tears off his face.

Hellinger *to the representatives:* Thank you all.

Hellinger gets the man to sit next to him again.

Hellinger *to the man:* This is the real issue. We could see that your main concern is the care for your wife's organization for autistic children.

Who is autistic in your family?

Man: My son.

Hellinger: We could see your love for him.

To the group: I'll go back to this once more.

Hellinger places the man once again, and opposite him the autistic son's representative, four meters apart.

Hellinger *to the autistic son's representative:* Tell him: "Me for you."

Autistic Son: *Me for you.*

Hellinger: How did you feel when you said that to him?

Autistic Son: *I feel so much love for him.*

Hellinger chooses another representative and lets him take the place of the autistic son, who can sit down again.

Hellinger *to the man:* You tell him: "Me for you."

Man: Me for you.
Hellinger *to this representative:* Say *to the man:* "Thank you."
This Representative: *Thank you .*

The two go towards each other. They stand side by side and look to the ground. After a while, this representative puts his head on the man's shoulder. The man holds him, without embracing him.

Hellinger gets the mine's representative to come back onto the stage. The man goes towards her. He embraces her with one arm. With his other hand, he holds the other representative and pulls him along with him. After a while the man lets go of this representative's hand and embraces the mine with both arms.

Hellinger *to the representatives:* Thank you all.

To the group: I will give you an explanation on the background of what we could see here just now. Why did I let the autistic son's representative say to his father: "Me for you"? I perceived that the father was afraid to become autistic, and that the son had taken it on for him, unconsciously, out of love for him. We often see such dynamics in family constellations. At the same time I also perceived that the father, too, had taken on the fear of becoming autistic, from someone of an earlier generation. Therefore I placed another representative for an autistic person, to whom the father had said inside: "Me for you." This other one felt relieved through thus. Therefore he said to him: "Thank you." So, everywhere, a

secret love is at work, that is prepared to take on a burdened fate for someone else.
To the man: Now back to you again. How do you feel now?

Man: I think, the mine represented my mother.

Hellinger: May be. My question is: How do you feel about this new enterprise? This is a course about enterprises.

Man: I am prepared to start this new enterprise, but I still feel some reticence and concern in me.

Hellinger: This is about a big enterprise. The strength for this new enterprise comes from your autistic son. Here it shows that this enterprise serves something greater, regardless of what it costs you and what you may gain from it. This is about another love. Therefore you can trust: It will be successful. All right?

The man nods and says thanks Hellinger . The group claps.

Hellinger *to the group:* Normally I make a clear distinction between the work I do otherwise, that is, looking for the right order in families, and this work here, with enterprises. Here we cannot tell them apart all that clearly.

Meditation

Just close your eyes. I take you into a meditation. We look at our enterprise, at our work, at our profession, and we sense in us the inner movement, to which our enterprise, and our work, and our profession respond. Do they move away from us, or do they come towards us with love? Can we go towards them with love, cheerful and fulfilled? Do we know and sense ourselves in the service of life, together with them, in a movement that brings other people happiness? Or do we perhaps feel drawn to a dead person, or to someone whom we and our family have excluded? Perhaps because we and our family felt guilty towards this person?

Now we look at these people with love. We open our heart for them, and we give them a place in our love and in our life, and we say to them: Yes. Now, connected with them in this way, we look at our enterprise again, at our work, at our profession. As we said yes to those whom we excluded from our love, we say yes to our enterprise, to our work, to our profession. We say yes to them with love, and we feel the difference, in our strength, in the new energy in us.

Further examples on this topic you'll find under:

Orders of rank:
Second example:
Business partners
The order of siblings 70

Money:
SECOND EXAMPLE:
Ruin.....................98

Double displacement:
Sexuality and death...... 139

Third topic

The victims

Introductory remarks

Which victims?

The victims I am here referring to are those at whose expense we and our enterprise profited. These victims may have incurred damage and loss or even death. This could have happened even before our time, so that we were not personally involved in their damage and loss and even death, and therefore not guilty. We might not even have known about these victims when we joined the enterprise.

Reversely this also means, that others had an advantage for their enterprise, at our expense, at our loss, that we became their victims.

So we have events that left are winners and losers behind, or where direct conflict was involved, victorious and defeated ones. Then there are also those who made room for others, at the expense of their own fate, or those who perhaps still do, so that others profit from their loss. And then there are those, who were not involved in the fate of the people who incurred these losses – even the loss of their lives –, but they still benefit from these people's losses.

The question is: Can we, for instance, in the first case, keep this profit? Or do we pay a price for it, one way or another, often a high price?

The other question is: We have given something our full effort, yet it comes to light that our successes do not come. Then what is missing for them, that would allow them to come and stay with us?

We form a community of fate with those, through whose sacrifice we gain. We are also in a community of fate with those who had an advantage through our loss or damage or our premature departure, who gained success through our lack of it.

Let's go to the first question. Not every gain is ours, not every enterprise either. It sometimes shows in a constellation, that an enterprise wants to go to someone else. A house that we bought in good faith, sometimes wants to belong to another person. We cannot live in it without suffering in some way.

Something needs to be done in such a situation, so that all involved can feel good, we, the house, the former owner, What it is, depends on the particular situation, and we can find this out through a constellation. May be we have to hand the house back to its rightful owner. May be we have to abandon it, or else we get entangled in something that happened in this house, something that will make people sick who live in it later, or harm them and their children in some other way.

The same goes for an enterprise. The earlier victims need to be reconciled. This can happen when the enterprise is run with those in mind who made way or had to make way, when it is run in the service of a concern shared by both sides. Including the former victims in something that considers them, allows them to agree to their fate willingly. With this, they are connected to the new owners in goodwill, and they can bless their success.

From hereon, such an enterprise is run in humility, with a sense of for the time being, without being presumptuous. It is run as a service, also in the service of its employees and their families. In the end, such an enterprise is sometimes handed over to its own fate. It is guided by other powers, taken elsewhere, towards peace for all.

Reversely, how is it, when others had an advantage through our fate? Worse still, when they were partly responsible for our suffering and loss, and they gloat about it, secretly or even openly?

For instance, do we want to get our property back from them, do we want to enforce this through prolonged legal action? What we lost, does it want to come back to us after that? If we get it back, does it want to stay with us? Can damage really be repaired this way? Or does it become damage and burden for both sides, as in reparations?

All attempts of this kind have something in common: they look back, instead of ahead.

What happens to those who gained at our expense, we leave up to them. It becomes their fate.

In looking forward, we are freed of our past losses, so that we can succeed in something new, often way beyond what we lost. At the same time, this also frees us from the fate of those who profited. We leave them to their gains without regret or reproach. They master their fate in their way. And we are and remain in our full strength. How? Successfully.

What is behind this attitude? What is at work in it, what in it becomes a blessing for many? In everything, we see another power at work, beyond gain and loss, beyond guilt and innocence, beyond perpetrators and victims. We submit to this power, whatever the result will be, for us and for others.

No one can survive, other than at the expense of others, in small as in big matters. We willingly pay our share and agree to the share it costs others. They and us, we are in the same service, in a changing interplay, in the service of life with love.

Example: *Every man for himself*

From a course in Moscow • 20. – 21. Mai 2009

Hellinger *to a man:* What kind of enterprise is it?
Man: I publish a journal on psychology. I also have another enterprise that finances the journal. This journal is a social project for me.

Hellinger: What kind of enterprise is the other one?
Man: It processes gold. With the profit I finance this journal.

Hellinger: Okay, come here and sit next to me. What does this enterprise manufacture?
Man: It manufactures and sells jewelry.

Hellinger: So it's about manufacturing jewelry. How's the enterprise doing?
Man: The enterprise is working, but there are problems that interfere with work.

Hellinger: What are these problems?
Man: Through this work, the enterprise makes a lot of profit, but on the other hand, I am fearful, in doing this job.

Hellinger: What are these fears?
Man: I am afraid to end up in jail. I'm afraid of the police. I'm afraid of criminals.

Hellinger: Whom does the enterprise serve? One you have mentioned. It serves also this journal.
Man: It serves my family and it serves the employees and those who buy something from us.

Hellinger: How many employees do you have?
Man: About 400 employees.

Hellinger: When you think of that, an enterprise that has 400 employees, how many families does it serve directly! I visualize that. That is a great service, because the life of many people depends on it. Therefore we will do our best, to help the enterprise and all the people it serves.

Okay, let's start. We will simply have a look at it, with the help of family-constellations. This means I will set this up with the help of representatives. Then we will see from their movements, what kind pf problem this enterprise has.

Hellinger chooses a representative for this man, a female representative for his enterprise, and he places them opposite each other, at some distance.

The man backs away from the enterprise more and more. The enterprise reaches the right hand out to him, as if it wanted to point at him. The man backs away even further, and is close to falling over backwards

HELLINGER *to the man:* Your representative is afraid of the enterprise.

Hellinger chooses three men. They stand next to each other, between the enterprise and the man, but to the side, about three meters away from the centre line.

HELLINGER *to these men:* You represent those who also profit from the enterprise. It appears, there are others making money from it also.

One of these men goes slowly towards the enterprise. The enterprise leans to the left, away from him, and falls to the ground.

The man's representative leans away form these men in the same direction, and also falls to the ground.

One of the three men stands next to the enterprise and looks down on it. He kicks the enterprise, pushes it away, and stomps his feet. Then he stands over the enterprise, so that it is lying between his feet. The enterprise groans with fear.

The man's representative lies on his back and puts both his hands over his mouth.

HELLINGER *to the man:* The enterprise is afraid of this man. He is the owner, the secret owner.

After a while: The business cannot survive. And especially you can't survive here. This is danger for your life. Your fears are justified.

Hellinger shows to the man's representative, who closes his mouth with both his hands.

HELLINGER *to the man:* You are not allowed to say anything, even though you know it. We see it in his movement. You haven't got a say here at all. You are at the mercy of other powers

MAN: Does it mean I have to give the enterprise up?

HELLINGER: If you want to stay alive, there is not other way. Let go of your business, your life is at stake.

The man nods.

Hellinger goes to the man's representative who is still lying on the ground, and he asks him how he is.
The Man's Representative: *I am shaking heavily. I am terribly afraid. It is very hard for me, what's going on there. It is hard for me, all the things this man does. I want to interfere, but my fear is too great. I have to go along with it. I just have to obey.*

Hellinger lifts the man up and places him opposite the business and the other man.

Hellinger *to the man:* You are also afraid that the business can be blackmailed. The business can be blackmailed, very badly. Perhaps it would be the right thing to do to move to another country.
The Man's Representative: *This here is very dangerous.*

Hellinger takes him by the hand and leads him away from the others, a long way outside.

Hellinger: How is this?
The Man's Representative *points forward:* I must go even further.

Hellinger: Okay. That's it.
To the representatives: Thank you all.

Clapping in the group

Following a hint from Sophie, Hellinger places the man's representative opposite his business, well away from the others.

Hellinger *to the group:* This would be his business in another country.

The man goes towards his business. Then he signals to Hellinger and says: Here I am much better. But there's still something, coming from behind and from the left.

Sophie Hellinger chooses another woman and puts her in the place of the old business in front of the man.

The Man's Representative: This is much better.

Hellinger *to the man:* Sophie says: It must be a totally new business. The old business cannot come along. You must start all over again.

Sophie *after having asked several other representatives, to the man:* This means you must go to another country. For a while, you must not do anything. Then you can start again with the same idea, but with completely new people.

Clapping in the group

Hellinger *to the man:* What the constellation showed here, is that you were dragged into underhand dealings that are dangerous. The solution would be the complete break with what you did, the completely new beginning with a business that really serves the people, like your magazine, for instance. That's an enterprise that serves people.

SOPHIE HELLINGER: The most dangerous idea for my survival is, when I start business or a company, in order to have more and more money for myself. Then I am in the foreground with the idea, I don't have enough. The idea that I have very little, drives me on to more and more. Others can feel that, that I don't really want to serve anyone else, that I rather feel, other must serve me. In our time this idea for an enterprise is the most dangerous one, for health, for the family, the wife, the children, everyone. Everyone is drawn into that.

HELLINGER *to the group:* We only worked for a short time. In twenty minutes, everything important came to light. Is there a more efficient method, to understand what is most important in a short time? To have such deep insights that it can be lifesaving and open new perspectives?

HELLINGER *to the man:* Okay, all the best to you

Clapping in the group

Fourth topic

The orders of rank

Introductory remarks

The right place

The right place follows an order. We can neither choose nor conquer it. We can't give it away or lose it, either. It obeys a higher order that allocates the right place to everyone, that creatively allocates our right place to us all individually. Only in the right place, everyone and everything is in tune with the creative power that also creates and provides order – successfully in tune with it.

In the sphere of business this order of rank is often violated, with far reaching consequences for its success.

Men and women

In some cultures and circles men are given priority of rank over women. So in many families the first born boy is considered the firstborn child, even if he has an older sister, or several of them. Later on, if he is taking on the parent's business as the preferred heir, a constellation sometimes shows that this business would prefer to go to the older sister instead of him. In that case, for the business to remain successful, he must cede to his sister the priority that is rightfully hers, and he must take the place that it his in the order of rank, a second or even lower one.

The employees of this business breathe deeply after that. Now they feel that they themselves and their workplace are embedded in a good order. This increases their willingness to give their best effort.

So this does play an important role in family businesses, when it comes to passing it on to the next generation.

The founder

It's different when someone founds their own enterprise. The founder of an enterprise always holds the first place.

Is he or she allowed then to brings someone else from the family into the business, perhaps even in an equal or leading position?

In an enterprise the same order of rank applies as in the family. The founder of an enterprise takes the first place in the enterprise, in the same way as in a family the parents relate to the children. The founder is the creator of the enterprise. The business becomes something like a child to the founder. Therefore, nobody can dispute the founder's place as the first place, or share this place with the founder.

In the family of origin, the founder has a certain place, as one of the children, taking up the position according to the right place in the line of siblings, for instance the second or third one.

When other family members are included in the enterprise, there can be a conflict between the two systems, the business system and the family system.

Where the founder's father takes on an important role in this business, the father's role is still second to that of the founder. Even though the father holds the first place in the family, within the business he hands it over to the founder. A conflict between the systems is avoided, when the different orders of rank in one system as well as in the other system are acknowledged and complied with.

Where the founder includes an older sibling in the business and give this sibling a leading position, the conflict becomes unavoidable. As the founder, the entrepreneur is of higher rank than the sibling, on the other hand, the entrepreneur is of a lower rank as a later-born child. Often the older sibling behaves as if he or she were also of higher rank in the business, higher than the founder, even though here, the sibling has to accept a lower rank. A conflict of this nature will not arise when younger siblings become part of the business.

I hope you don't get bored when I still enlarge further on the orders of rank in an enterprise. They play a decisive role for success or failure. The following example will bring this light, perhaps shockingly so, for many.

Husband and wife

Whether we want to believe it or not, observations shows: As a rule, a family fares better if the man occupies the first place, if the wife and the children follow the man, here even in the literal sense. This becomes particularly clear when the man and the woman come from different countries, from different cultures and languages. Following means here, wife and children follow the father of the family into his country and language.

Obviously there are valid exceptions, but as the basic movement, this rule needs to be noted and observed.

Following does not at all mean, to obey, to let the man rule, for in this sense both parents are equal. Within the family is it usually the woman that leads, and the man serves and follows her.

After this introduction, we come to the aspect of the husband-wife relationship that concerns us here.

When a woman has started her own business, or when her parents passed their business on to her, she takes the first place in this business, even in relationship to her husband. Is she allowed to give her husband a role in her business? Perhaps a role equal to hers, or even a leading role?

No, for observation shows – I have not seen an exception yet: In the end a husband ruins his wife's business.

We can speculate what is behind this. So here are some more observations and assumptions.

Presumption

Those who want to take on a higher position and rank in an enterprise than what is appropriate for them, will fail. Violation of the order of rank is the major cause for ruin in many fields. Every tragedy begins with a violation of the order of rank.

What does this mean in family relationships? Someone who holds a lower place in the order of rank, like a child for instance, tries to help someone who is higher up in the order of rank. For instance, mother or father.

The same goes for an enterprise. Someone of lower rank, – someone who came later for instance –, who wants to take the first place by edging out the legitimate occupant of this position, will take the enterprise into ruin. To save the business, this person needs to be speedily replaced by someone who respects the order.

Now we return to the husband and wife relationship. If a man it taken into his wife's business, for instance in an equal position, it won't be long until he takes the first position in it, internally and externally, because that's what he is used to in his family. But he does not succeed in it. Especially in the eyes of the employees he always remains number two. The business doesn't want him either. The only power left to him is the power to destroy.

I exaggerate of course, but concerning the order of rank, the ultimate is at stake. It is a matter of life and death, in a business, too.

This is not the case when a woman joins her husband's business and takes on an equal position there. From the order in the family she is used to taking the second place. She is in harmony with it, and still she can feel an equal there. Her contribution to the business is felt as beneficial, and the employees treat her as an equal to her husband.

Siblings

When several siblings jointly take on an enterprise from their parents, the sibling order of rank applies. So, the first child, whether it is male or female, takes the first position, and with it the leading role. The others follow according to their rank of age.

Here is applies again: the husbands of the sisters remain outside. The wives of the brothers can be included, only together with their husbands, though, without taking on a position of rank themselves.

But it does make a difference if one of the siblings has a special talent and therefore takes on a leading role in the enterprise. Here it shows that in this enterprise a second order of rank needs to be acknowledged, the order of rank according to personal capacity and the achievement resulting from it.

The twofold order of rank

In a clinic, so it appears, the doctors come first, and after them the medical assistance, and other specialists. In a constellation one can find out immediately, where the appropriate right place is for every individual in the whole team.

Before the doctors comes the administration. Similar to the man in the family, the administration is responsible for safeguarding the enterprise towards the outside and for the economic base on which it rests, and on which the smooth running of the clinic depends.

So there is an order of rank according to the roles and to their importance for the successful running of the enterprise. And within the different departments there is still the order of rank according to the duration of membership. Both these orders need to be observed side by side and together, simultaneously.

For instance when someone takes on the first position in leadership, but the last one in duration of membership in this team, he or she has the first place in regards to leading the enterprise. Concerning the relationships in the team, having joined last, they have the last position. Behaving accordingly in the human aspect, as someone who came last, they can be assured of the staff's helpfulness. The question is: Do they lead less successfully or more so? They know themselves more supported from below.

In the reverse, the double order of rank also exists amongst the staff. Who has served this enterprise the longest, deserves due respect. Nobody who came later can dispute this position. Nevertheless, long serving members still have to earn this place through corresponding effort and achievement. If they slacken off, the higher rank according to length of serving does not protect them from the consequences of decreasing achievement. In a enterprise achievement comes first.

So much as an overview. The following examples will expand on this and deepen our understanding.

The order of life

The order of rank is a basic order of life in all fields. The consequences of obeying or violating it we can most clearly observe in enterprises, in their success or failure. Here above all, the order of rank reveals itself as a basic order of life, if you like, as an irreversible divine law, deciding over life an death. For the consequences of violating this order of rank, are brought home to us in every tragedy, the death of the hero, his failure, for himself and for those whom he sweeps away with him.

What protects us and our enterprises from this fate? The right place. The right place makes us safe and strong and also connected, successfully connected.

First example:
The priority of the employees

From the course in Curitiba, Brazil • 19. – 20. August 2008

Hellinger: I'll continue with the topic: "Success in organizations". There are specific situations, for instance where husband and wife have a business together. And we can have a look at this, when we have people here, who have a business as husband and wife.

A woman puts up her hand and sits next to Hellinger .

HELLINGER: What kind of a business is it?
WOMAN: It's about food that we distribute to different industries who work with food.

HELLINGER: To whom does the business belong?
WOMAN: The business belongs to my husband. We work together. I've only been in the business for the last one and a half years. He founded the business.

HELLINGER: Are there any problems?
WOMAN: I in the personnel department. I see the difficultly for a real team to form, that people stay in the business and don't leave again. It's like that, there are always people coming and going, always new staff.

HELLINGER: The question is: What effect does an ongoing turnover of staff have? I don't want to know this right now. We will have a look at it.

In a business several factors play a role. The first one is the product. The second one are the customers, the third one the staff members, and the fourth one the profit. Are there also shareholders?
WOMAN: No.

Hellinger: So, now we will look at this business. You stand there for the owner. Put yourself into your husband's place and stand there.

The woman takes her place as her husband's representative.

The Hellinger chooses a female representative and places her to the left of the owner. Next, he chooses two women and a man as the representatives for the staff. They stand next to each other, opposite the owner and the business, about five meters away.

Then he chooses a female representative for the profit, for the money. This representative stands at some distance, inside left to the business.

Next he chooses two female representatives for the customers, and places them at some distance to the right of the staff.

Hellinger: Okay, let's have a look

The customers slowly move towards the owner, in very small steps. They stand closely opposite him, and after a while to the left and to the right of him. Together, they go backwards, away from the employees. They look at each other again and again. Then they hold each other by the hands.

The business took a few steps back and stands there, isolated.

The money has its eyes firmly on the employees.

Hellinger: From the movement we see, the business is oriented towards the customers. At whom does the money look?

After a while: The money is always looking at the employees. They do not feel good. They feel neglected.

The money moves its hands restlessly. A female customer moves towards the employees, briefly reaches her hands out to them and sways her head from side to side.

A female employee has turned away and taken a few steps away from the others.

Hellinger after a while to the business: How is the business?
Business: I am somewhat lost.
Hellinger *to the group:* Whom does a business support? The employees! And whom do the employees support? The business!

The owner has moved further away from the business, to the right. Parallel to her stands a female employee but they have not moves closer to each other. But they look towards each other.

Hellinger *to the group:* I'll try something out.

Hellinger takes the business to the front. To her right, he places the owner. To the left of the business he places the money, and to the left of the money he places the employees. They all stand next to each other. The he places the customers opposite them at some distance.

Hellinger asks the employees how they are now.

First Employee: *Better.*

Second Employee: *Better.*

Third Employee *who had turned and gone away: Much lighter.*

Hellinger to the owner's representative: All the employees are there together for the customers, only when they are together, are they there for the business.

How is the business now?

Business: *Better.*

Hellinger: How's the money?

Money: Very good.

Hellinger *to the group:* This is a team that is there for the customers. When only the customers are seen, the employees are sacrificed to the customers. The money did not feel well, because it doesn't go where it needs to go first. It must go to the employees.

To the owner's representative: Your employees are poorly paid. That's why they come and go. They do the work and they are not acknowledged. Is it clear to you?

The Owner's Wife: *This is an ongoing discussion between me and my husband. He works in the finances of the business and I work in the personnel department. He is very concerned about the sales and I care about the employees. That's our conflict.*

Hellinger: Selling doesn't work without the employees. The employees have priority. Is it clear to you?

The Owner's Wife: *Yes.*

Hellinger: I leave it here. You can sit down again.
To the group: I'll take a representative for the man as well.

Hellinger chooses a representative for the owner and places him opposite his wife, at some distance.

Both look at each other. The man has his hands folded behind his back.

Hellinger chooses a female representative for the business again and places her in the spot of the wife. He gets the wife to sit next to him again.

The Man: Suddenly my heart began to beat really fast.
Hellinger: Better or worse?
The Man: Better.

Hellinger to the wife: You must leave the business to your husband.

How is the business?
Business: Better here.
Hellinger *to the representative:* Okay, thank you.
To the group: I'll tell you some personal experiences. My first wife and I offered therapy together. Sometimes we were fighting all of a sudden. We didn't know where that came from.

The background was, there was a conflict concerning a client. She represented one concern of the client, and I another one. Suddenly we noticed, that the conflict they had was transferred on us, because we focused on the different sides.

Here we have the same danger. When husband and wife run the same business, there are conflicts within the business. These conflicts are transferred to the personal relationship – and vice versa. The personal conflicts are also transferred to the business. I just offer you this to think about.

To the woman: Okay?

WOMAN: The situation was, he asked me to join him. I was a psychologist and worked in a practice. He wanted me to work with him, because the business had grown a lot. But perhaps this is just a phase, perhaps I was only meant to work with him for a time?

HELLINGER: It is better when you stay in your own profession and he in his. Then you have a lot to talk about in the evening.

The woman and the whole group laugh.

SECOND EXAMPLE: *Business partners*

From the course in Moscow • 20. – 21. May 2009

HELLINGER: Okay, let's continue.

To a woman: What kind of a business is it about?

WOMAN: It's about textiles.

HELLINGER: How many employees do you have?

Woman: 500.

Hellinger: What is the problem at the moment?
Woman: There are difficulties with running the business.

Hellinger: Whose business is it?
Woman: There are two owners. That's my sister and me.

Hellinger: The two of you are the owners?
Woman: Yes.

Hellinger: Which one of you is older?
Woman: My sister is older. I am younger.

Hellinger: Who founded the business?
Woman: Me.

Hellinger: You founded it?
Woman: Yes.

Hellinger: What exactly is the difficulty now?
Woman: My sister and I, we are different, and we had intense conflict.

Hellinger: Where did the money for the business come from?
Woman: To some extent it was my sister's money. The biggest part came from me.

HELLINGER chooses representatives for this woman and her sister and places them side by side, the woman to the left of her sister. Then he places a female representative for the business opposite them.

The woman's representative goes to the business, and the business to her. The older sister moves away from the business and from her sister.

HELLINGER *to the woman:* Whose business is it, when you have a look at this here?
WOMAN: Mine.

HELLINGER: The business is yours, yours alone. You founded it. No one else can be on par with the founder later on. This is an order. So, pay your sister out and run the business on your own.
As she wants to reply: Wait a little.

Suddenly the woman bursts out laughing.

HELLINGER to the sister's representative: How is it for you here?
the sister's representative: I am better here.
HELLINGER *to the representatives:* Okay, that's it.

The order of rank

Hellinger *to the group:* The difficulty here comes about because an order of rank has been violated. The majority of difficulties in businesses arise from the violation of an order of rank. This order of rank is unknown. In our culture it is not known. It is one my great discoveries, having found this order of rank.

This order of rank determines which place an individual can have. Those who were there earlier have priority over those who came later. Also a product that was there first, has priority over products that come later.

The founder of a business has always got the first place. A founder cannot be replaced by anyone who will come later. When someone who came later wants to grab the first place, the business will suffer.

To this woman: As your sister is older, according to age she would have the first place. But this is not a family, this is a business. You founded it. You alone would have to run it. Your sister can work with you, but only in a subordinate position..

Of course this doesn't work here, evidently, because as your older sister she feels of a higher rank than you. So here we have two orders of rank.

To this woman: So the simplest solution is quite obvious: You give her the money back or you give here a share, but she can't stay in the business.

Woman: We had many attempts at separating.

Hellinger: That doesn't work. The best solution is, she takes her money and starts her own business. That's the best solution for everyone. In the constellation she felt better that way. You don't have to be against each other.

Sophie Hellinger: What you saw and felt and experienced here, is a new situation. Don't go back into the old one. Trust the constellation and wait, without doing anything. Don't talk about it with anyone. You let it grow in your soul, what you saw here.

Hellinger: Those of you who participated in the intensive course, understand: What Sophie suggested to her is: Doing through non-doing.

To this woman: Because you know . . .

The woman laughs loudly.

Hellinger: You like that… Something is also happening with your sister. This constellation has also an immediate effect on your sister. You only have to wait.

Sophie Hellinger: To your sister as your sister, not as your business partner, you say on the personal level, but only inside: "I'm the little one, you are the big one." You take care of yourself, on your own.

Hellinger: The younger sister must not help the older sister. That violates the order of rank in the family.

The woman is very moved by this and cries.

Sophie Hellinger: If you worry about her, nothing works. It does not work together and it does not work apart. Close your eyes. Inside, say to her: "My mummy is also your mummy. I remain just your little sister. Concerning the work, I'll show you all, how big I am."

The woman laughs and wipes her tears away.

Hellinger *to the woman:* How are you now?
Woman: I am very sad.
Hellinger: Ah yes?

The order of siblings

Sophie places the sibling line. She places the woman to the left of her big sister. She hears that the woman had a younger brother who died. She chooses a representative for the woman's younger brother and places him on her left side.

Sophie *to the woman:* Look at your sister and say to her: "You are the big one."

Woman: You are the big one.

The sister nods. The sisters look at each other for a long time.

Sophie places the sister's representative a bit further away. The dead brother's representative wants to sit down, but she tells him to remain standing, even though he is dead. Then she chooses another female representative and places her between the woman and the bigger sister.

Sophie *to the woman:* How are you now?
Woman: I feel a bit lighter.
Sophie *to the big sister's representative:* How is it for you?
The Big Sister's Representative: I have the feeling there is someone else who needs to stand left of me.

Sophie chooses another woman and places her to the left of the big sister. The woman and her younger brother stand with their arms around each other's shoulder.

Sophie *to the big sister's representative:* How are you now?
The big Sister's Representative: *I feel better.*

All the siblings feel good now. Sophie gets one after the other to say: I am the first. I am the second. I am the third. I am the fourth. I am the fifth. The dead brother also feels good. He and the woman look at each other with love.

Hellinger *to the woman:* Your brother would be the right business partner for you.

Hellinger *to the woman, once she sits between him and Sophie again:* How are you now?

Woman *laughs:* Very good.

Hellinger *to the group:* What we could see here: Without understanding the laws of relationships in families, and how they have their effect in our whole life, we cannot be in control of a business. Many issues have their cause in something important in the family. Dead siblings for instance, or aborted siblings, one's own aborted children also have an immediate effect on the business.

Hellinger *to the woman:* All the best.

The orders

From the course about laws of success in business in São Paulo · 31.3. – 1.4. 2009

HELLINGER: I have thought about what goes on in businesses. The same as in real life, when you look at it. Businesses are a part of real life.

Life is moved by a power. Everything is moved by a power, by a power that moves things on, and also by a power that holds on to us and attracts us, gravity for instance.

Everything that moves, moves in accordance with an order. When we deviate from an order in our life, a counterforce brings us back into a direction that goes further. When a pendulum swings in one direction, a force also pulls it back. The pendulum swings back and forth over a centre. In this centre energy collects. But even the centre is in motion, as all of creation in constantly moving. It appears as if it was in a circular movement, so that it always encircles a centre.

This movement is a knowing movement. Therefore it is a spiritual movement. Sometimes we distinguish thoughtlessly between material and spiritual. For instance we differentiate between our body and our spirit, and we consider our body to be something material. But the body is spiritually influenced any moment. When we have an insight, for instance, a spiritual insight, it has an immediate effect on our body. The insight takes our body along into a spiritual movement, into a creative movement.

Why do I say all this, given that this is a course about businesses and organizations? A spiritual movement is at work there as well, a movement of order, in the service of life. So we look at a business as a movement of life, and we find out if it serves life, and to what extent.

When a business deviates from an order of life, like when the pendulum goes too far in one direction, for instance into the direction of profit, it will swing in the other direction after a while. In the end the pendulum oscillates around the one centre.

The same applies in reverse. When the pendulum has gone too far in the other direction, towards charity for instance, it will also swing back. So as we move in an enterprise, every movement has its meaning, and all the movements must find an order of working together in a balanced way, they must find their order in the greater whole.

What these orders are, we get to see in these constellations, step by step. The orders themselves are also in motion. These movements always serve the same purpose. They serve the fulfillment of life. In this sense we continue our work here today, in the service of enterprises and in the service of life.

Third example: *Amalgamations*

From the course about laws of success in business in São Paulo • 31.3. – 1.4. 2009

***Hellinger** to a man:* What is the issue?
Man: I have a company, and today, the 1.April, we join our company with two other companies, we amalgamate. The amalgamation is only in the economic sector. There are three companies that have the same clientele. I am responsible for this business sector. This business sector that is amalgamated now, has to market the product of these three companies.

Hellinger: Who initiated the movement towards amalgamation?
Man: I did.

Hellinger: Do the others agree?
Man: They agree. In the beginning of the amalgamation, I only envisaged the fusion with one company. Then another company came and made an offer to join in the amalgamation.

Hellinger: Who gains from the amalgamation?
Man: The other companies gain, and the customers, too.

Hellinger: And the employees?
Man: The structure will be different somehow.

Hellinger: My question was more precise.
Man: The employees will be integrated in this new model.

Hellinger: Do they gain something through this, or do they lose ?
Man: Some employees will personally lose something, others will gain.

Hellinger: What does it mean, lose?
Man: Some will lose something.

Hellinger: Some will lose their work, to put it clearly. So, the gain comes at the expense of others. I just describe it, without assessing it.
Man: In this moment it is possible for this to happen, of course, but because we expand, new employees can also be taken on.

Hellinger: We will have a look what effect this has. What effect it has on the company itself. I have a certain image, from the dynamics, the effect it will have on the employees. Also the effect it will have on the productivity of the employees that will stay on. These are deliberations that have their place of course. In this sense, I see the company as a movement of life. The question is, to what extent does it serve life or perhaps also oppose life in a

certain way? The question is, what has priority here? In this way, we would have a look at it. Is that all right?
MAN: Yes.

HELLINGER: The question is, how do we gain this insight? How would we proceed here? I'll begin with the obvious.

I will place representatives for the three companies.
MAN: One of these companies that will join this amalgamation, used to be a competitor of ours. Now it joins this union.

HELLINGER: This is probably an advantage for all.
MAN: Yes.

HELLINGER: We just have a look at it. I don't want to know who these companies are, I just take one, two, three. You know what is one, what is two, what is three. As I only concentrate on the relationships, I don't need to know any details. I stay completely within my sphere, the sphere of relationships. With any other questions I leave the know-how where it belongs. I am consulted here concerning relationships, and the orders in relationships. Therefore you can feel safe with me. I don't meddle in things where you are an expert. This delineation is important. Okay so far?
MAN: Yes.

HELLINGER: Now you choose a representative for the company number one, then for two, then for three, and you place them in relationship to each other, just from your feeling.

He places them in a triangle. The second to the left of the first, but a bit more in front. The third company opposite both of them.

HELLINGER *to the representatives:* Let a movement take you. We watch how the movement goes.

The second company moves on tiptoes. The third company takes one step backwards. Later on it takes several steps back and turns away from the others. It looks back for a moment and then goes even further away. The two other companies have come closer. The third company takes another step back, but then, another one forward.

Hellinger asks the man, to join them as the representative for the profit.

The second company becomes more and more restless. The third company is unsure whether to go backward or away. It is also quite restless.

The profit does not know where to go, and it looks outside.

HELLINGER *after a while to the first company:* How are you?
FIRST COMPANY: I feel in accord with the second company. I would like the profit to make contact with us.
HELLINGER *to the second company:* How are you?
second company: I feel very powerful and seductive. I sense that I have a lot of power, and I know that power attracts me.
HELLINGER to the profit: How is it with you?

The Profit: I feel attracted to the whole thing, but I don't know in which direction to go.
Hellinger to the third company: With you?
Third Company: *I am like paralyzed. My feet hurt a lot. I can neither go forwards nor backwards. I don't have any contact with what's behind me.*

Hellinger takes the third company some steps forward.

Hellinger to the first company: How is it for you now?
First Company: I don't care at all, whether I am with him or with him. But the other one there I don't need.
Hellinger to the second company: And you?
second company: I feel relieved. Now I can look into the future.
Hellinger to the profit: And you?
The Profit: *Now I am looking for a place for me.*

Hellinger: Do.

The profit slowly turns in a circle. Doing this, he moves away from companies one and two. The third company looks back at the profit. Then the profit looks outside.

Hellinger *to the group:* This simple movement shows: The profit for the companies one and two is lost through company three. Because the profit looks there instead of at those there. Here a hidden law comes to light. I'll explain it later.

Hellinger chooses another representative and places him at some distance to the right of the third company, but facing the profit and the two other companies.

HELLINGER: You are a fourth company that also joins in.

The third company has turned around and now stands next to the fourth company. So on one side the first and the second company stand next to each other, on the other side the third and the fourth. The profit stands in between them.

HELLINGER *to the first company:* How are you now?
FIRST COMPANY: *I like this idea.*
SECOND COMPANY: I don't like it that much.
HELLINGER *to the group:* He is losing power that way.
To the third company: And how are you now?
THIRD COMPANY: This is quite pleasant.
HELLINGER to the fourth company: How are you?
FOURTH COMPANY: I am still confused.
HELLINGER to the profit: How is it for you now?
THE PROFIT: I'm turning in circles here, but I am attracted by all sides.

HELLINGER *to the man for whom he did this constellation:* I'll explain the law. When you have three, one has to go. You take either two or four, but never three. To save this amalgamation, a fourth company must join. A committee of three is a bad committee, be-

cause two are always against a third. This is a law of life. When you know this, one can save a fortune.
MAN: I am open to find one more or to let go of one.

HELLINGER: The movement of life goes always towards more. As soon as you send one away, the others weaken. You must bring in a fourth one. Expansion is a movement of life. I leave it here. I think I have shown something important.
MAN: Thank you.
HELLINGER *to the representatives:* Thank you all.

Hellinger asks the man to sit next to him again.

HELLINGER: This is an order, an order of life.
MAN: There is so much light all of a sudden.

HELLINGER: Exactly. You are fine now.

The man nods.

HELLINGER: The other consideration, concerning the employees, I leave aside now, the effect it has on the employees, for instance when there is a hostile takeover. A hostile takeover can never succeed, never. The employees who are taken over by another company, do not feel the same connection with their company any more. A company lives on the employees' loyalty and on the employees' ability to identify with their company. Employees never identify

with shareholders. These are very simple laws. But now you have understood a lot about that. Can I leave it there?
Man: Yes.

Hellinger: All the best to you.

The majority

Hellinger: Any questions about this perhaps?
A Man: When there are four, it is difficult to get a majority. It often happens then, that there is a conflict of two against two.

Hellinger: The majority is in the way of success, because for every majority there is a minority. The minority prevents the success of the majority.

Now I've mentioned another basic law. It matters to find a consensus amongst all. The outsider who appears to prevent something, forces all to look for a new, more encompassing solution. So it makes a difference, whether one works with majorities, or whether one comes into a movement that includes and considers all.

Fourth example:
The solution

From the course about the laws of success' in Vladivostok • 3. – 4. June 2009

***Hellinger** to a woman:* What kind of an enterprise is it?
Woman: A commercial enterprise.

Hellinger: How many employees do you have?
Woman: About 120.

Hellinger: So what exactly is your issue?
Woman: I don't really have a specific problem. Generally, everything is normal.

Hellinger: Is the enterprise successful?
Woman: Reasonably, yes.

Hellinger: Who owns the enterprise?
Woman: Three owners who make decisions.

Hellinger: How do the owners get on?
Woman: Good.

Hellinger: Who started the enterprise?

Woman: Me, and another owner. Then a third one joined in with his enterprise.

Hellinger: How did this third one join?
Woman: He brought an added direction into the enterprise, a further option how to develop the business.

Hellinger: How is the profit distributed?
Woman: The shard business is distributed according to the percentages. What we achieve together is shared equally.

Hellinger: Shared equally?
Woman: No, not like that.

Hellinger: So how then?
Woman: 38 – 38 – 24 per cent.

Hellinger: Who gets the 24%?
Woman: The third one.

Hellinger: Okay. If there are no problems, I don't have to solve any. But I have a look at it, just so. Yes?
Woman: You did say, that it is also about how our enterprise will develop further in the future. Right now everything is okay, but I would like to know how my business will develop further?

Hellinger: I will begin with some details. We can learn something from them. Is the second owner a woman?
Woman: Both other owners are men.

Hellinger: I will set up the relationship between the owners. Are you familiar with family constellations?
Woman: Yes, I am. Last year I also participated in the seminar.

Hellinger: I work with representatives, that's better. Then you only need to watch. Okay?
Woman: Yes.

Hellinger chooses a woman and two men as the representatives for the enterprise and places them facing each other in a triangle, at great distance between them all. Then he chooses a woman as the representative for the enterprise and places her in front of them, at a distance.

Hellinger *to the representatives:* You recollect yourselves, then you allow yourselves to be moved as you are being moved from inside. That way we get the essential information.

The third owner turns immediately to the enterprise. The enterprise goes a little to one side and looks at the other two owners. Then it goes back and turns to the outside, away from the owners.

The second owner want to stand next to the enterprise, but the enterprise moves away from him and stands opposite the third owner.

The first owner, the woman, remains in her place, away from the others.

HELLINGER *to the woman:* Where did the money for the enterprise come from?
WOMAN: We earned it together.

HELLINGER: Are you related or married to the second owner?
WOMAN: No.

HELLINGER: With whom lies the future? We see it lies with the third owner, and you withdraw.
To the group: In a few minutes we see the basic movement of the whole enterprise.
To the enterprise: How do you feel when the second owner stands behind you?
ENTERPRISE: *When he stood near me, I felt my arm, my hand was very heavy.*
HELLINGER: How do you mean, heavy – pleasant or unpleasant?
ENTERPRISE: *Unpleasant. There was pressure. My hand, my arm, they were uncomfortable.*

The third owner goes forward, past the enterprise, looking to the ground. The first owner goes towards the enterprise. It turns to her. Later, the third owner looks past the enterprise, into the distance.

HELLINGER: I need one more woman.

Hellinger chooses a woman for the enterprise that the third owner brought into the joint enterprise. Hellinger places it to the left of the third owner, at a distance, and away from anything else. The third owner goes to it. The enterprise stands behind him and holds him.

Hellinger turns him around to face the enterprise, so that they stand opposite. They take each other by the hands.

***Hellinger** to the large enterprise:* How are you now? Better or worse?

The large Enterprise: Better.

***Hellinger** to the second owner:* How are you?

Second Owner: Also better.

***Hellinger** to the first owner:* And you?

First Owner: Good.

***Hellinger** to the woman:* This amalgamation was a bad idea. Amalgamations are risky. You can work together, but not become one enterprise. Both enterprises must remain independent. Is it okay?

Woman: Yes.

Hellinger: More is not needed.

To the representatives: Thank you all.

Applause from the group

Hellinger *to the group:* The future of a big enterprise that provides the livelihood of many families depends on the knowledge of certain laws. These laws come to light here.
To the woman: You were lucky that it didn't go further. Like this it will be good

There was something else to observe. The one who joined last took on the leadership. He put himself in the first place. The other two were ousted in a way. They lost their strength. Now, all are in their strength. One can cooperate, that's the solution.
How are your employees doing then? Are they better or worse? Do they feel more connected with the enterprise or less? Employees are loyal to an enterprise. They form a field with it. In your enterprise they are loyal to the two of you. They form a field with you. They are more motivated if you remain independent. Just as the employees of the other enterprise are more motivated when they remain with that enterprise. Cooperation without amalgamation, that's the solution here. Then the order remains intact. If you had set this up, you would have saved yourself a lot of trouble. Is it okay like this?
Woman: Yes.
Hellinger: All the best!

A further example of this topic you find under:

The inheritance:

Fifth Topic

The money

Introductory remarks

Good money

The basic question in any business consultancy concerning success of failure: Where did the money come from that made it possible to start the business?

Was it money gained through one's one work? Did it come from an inheritance? Did it come from more than one person who owned a part of the business through their contribution? Did it come from a bank as a loan, or did it come from shareholders, who were hoping for a share in the profit they expected? Was it gained in an unlawful way, through fraud for instance, or did it just land in our lap, and we only had to take it? Where we gained, were there also losers, and what happened to them?

This list shows that we are dealing with a basic question that needs clarifying and answering, if an enterprise wants to be hel-ped

Money has a spiritual dimension. It responds as if it had a soul and a fine sense for justice and injustice.

It wants to stay with those who worked honestly to earn it, by the sweat of their brows, so to speak. It wants to return to those who came to it in this way, or to those, to whom it was given with the instruction to apply and to increase it honestly in the serve of life. The money that others earned for us wants to stay with us when we have paid them fairly. And generally, money belongs to life, and it wants to be spent and passed on in the service of life. Money is happy to be spent. All the richer will it return to us.

Are these just daydreams? Or do we observe it all the time, in many enterprises?

Why do entrepreneurs sometimes make mistakes that cost them a fortune, where other people can only shake their head in disbelief? The soul of the money was at work here.

Of course, to speak of the soul of money is a metaphor. Our own soul knows and senses what it must keep and what it must lose.

For the success of an enterprise it is important to assign money the place that is due to it. In a constellation for instance, we can see immediately, if the money wants to stay or to go. We also see where it wants to go. As a rule the business wants to go to the same place.

The question is, in such a situation, how do we get it to come back into our enterprise? What do we have to put into order so that it happily returns to us and stays with us?

Money shuns getting lost. It shuns getting lost wastefully, like to a gambler for instance. What does a gambler pay for with the lost money? One can see how many breathe a sigh of relief when they have lost their money. What have they gained for themselves with this loss? In such a situation, some say inside: " I rather gamble my money away than my life."

The same goes for an enterprise when its success is risked in a foolhardy way. Business consultancy turns into life consultancy, into survival consultancy.

How do business consultants relate to money in a successful way?

In the service of life, with respect and caution. This also applies to themselves. For instance, by asking as much money for their consultation as what this consultation successfully achieves in the end. In this way he is collaborating with the money, and – like the money – also with love.

A question to begin with

From the course in Vladivostok • 3. – 4. June 2009

Woman: Why is it so important in a constellation business, to ask where the money came from?

Hellinger: Sometimes it shows that the money wants to be elsewhere. For instance if it came from someone who is not respected. Or if it came through fraud. Then the money does not want to stay. Or when it comes to someone because someone else died. Then the money wants to stay with the dead person, unless that person is honored. Then the money wants to stay. This is an important question.

The other question is, whether the money serves the business. When the money primarily serves the shareholders, or when the whole business has to serve the shareholders, instead of it being the other way round, where the shareholders serve the business, then there will be a crisis.

First example: Where to with the money?

Woman: I have a question: When in a business the owners are married, and the wife is the manager and the husband the deputy, is there a violation of the hierarchy?

Hellinger: One has to look closely and distinguish clearly. Sometimes it is important that the partners have their own business. It is bad when the wife inherited a business, and her husband joins the business. Then the husband ruins the business. Reversely, when the husband is the owner and the wife takes on a leading role, it works well. These are the general rules. In individual cases there are differences. We can find it out quickly here. Was it a personal question you asked?
Woman: Yes.

Hellinger: Then we can have a look at it. What kind of a business is it?

Woman: A warehouse. We sell two kinds of merchandise: goods that are cheap, and expensive goods.

Hellinger: Which branch came first?
Woman: The cheap goods.

Hellinger: Which branch flourishes and which one doesn't?
Woman: Neither of them do well.

Hellinger: Okay, we'll have a look.

Hellinger chooses two women, one for the cheap goods, and one for the expensive ones, and he places them opposite each other. He chooses another woman as the representative for the warehouse. It looks at both, from 5 meters distance.

The representative for the cheap goods turns away. After a while she turns around fully and takes some steps forwards. The warehouse turns around. It does several circles on the spot, turns around again and moves a few steps away.

It doesn't find a place. Then it goes past the expensive goods and stands closer to the cheap goods. The expensive goods want to go to the warehouse first, but then they stop, and then they turn to the cheap goods and the warehouse which stands nearby.

Hellinger chooses three representatives for the customers. The warehouse wants to go towards them, but pauses. One of the customers has turned away. The cheap and the expensive goods both look at the customers without moving to them.

Now Hellinger chooses a female representative for the money and places her with the others. The warehouse immediately goes to the money and takes it by the hands. The expensive goods stand behind the warehouse. The cheap goods look at the customers, but these turn away.

HELLINGER *to the woman:* We have seen it.
To the representatives: Thank you!

To the group: What is money? Money is the nourishment that moves life on. It is the mother milk of life. It is given as a divine gift. It is there as a service so that we can stay alive. Some people want to hang on mother's breast their whole life long, always just taking.

Money serves. It has a soul, it is a thing. It serves life. Hard earned money serves life best. Therefore it plays a big role in a business where it came from. Money had a great need to serve. The deepest need money has, is to be spent and to be used in the service of life. Therefore it is so important to ask here: Where does the money come from?

Now we have an ancient Christian tradition. The believers are supposed to disrespect money. How is this with beggars? Does they respect money? How is it with poor people? Do they respect money? Money not respected is lost money.

Something else about good business. Good business is about fair and honest deals. They create trust and accordingly, attract more and more for new and greater gains. These gains stay.

Second example: *Ruin*

A woman: My question is connected to money. I have started successful businesses three times. But when the profit margin reached two million dollars, a disaster happened. For instance a ship burned, and I lost everything. This happened three times. Now I have written a business plan for a new enterprise. According to this plan, in two years time I will have a profit of 2 million dollars again. I am afraid to start this business, because of these two million dollars.

Hellinger: Shall we have a look at this? You just stand there.

She stands there herself. Hellinger chooses a representative for the money and places her 5 meters opposite from her.

The money looks to the ground and then to the side.
The woman takes a step backwards. Then it turns to the side. The money turns away further, until it has turned around fully, it goes forwards even a bit more, still looking to the ground.

Hellinger *to the group:* There isn't much that can be done here.

Hellinger chooses a representative and gets her to lie down unto the ground, with her back on the floor, behind the money. She represents a dead person. Then Hellinger turns the money towards this dead person. The client has also turned around,

The money lies down next to the dead person. The woman has come closer. Then she lies down on the other side of the dead person.

HELLINGER *to the group:* Where does this money want to go to? It wants to go to an aborted child. This is frequently the case, by the way, that a business represents an aborted child. These businesses perish.

The representative for the money gets up again and wants to turn away. Hellinger turns her around to the dead person again. The woman also gets up. She looks to the dead person with her hands folded behind her back.

HELLINGER *to the group:* The dead person is angry. She is angry. She clenches her fist.

The woman and the money squat in front of the dead person. The woman sits in front of her and looks at her. Then she strokes her face.

HELLINGER *to the group:* You realize what a deep soul money has? How alive money can be?

Hellinger chooses three representatives and gets them to lie down next to the dead person.

HELLINGER *to the group:* These are the three ruined businesses.

The money gets up, goes to the woman and puts her arms around her from the back. The dead person turns to them.

After a while the money pulls the woman off the ground and leads her away from the dead person. But the woman can't be pulls away. She goes to the dead person again.

Hellinger chooses a representative for the woman's newly planned business and places it at some distance behind her.

The woman stands behind this business and wants to lead it to the dead person. The money withdraws and sobs loudly.

The woman takes this business and goes back with it. She wants to lead it to the money. But the money has its arms crossed in front of its chest and turns away.

HELLINGER *to the group:* What we see here is that the feelings that should go to the child, have been transferred to the business. We can see, that businesses are connected to events in one's own family, and that something continues on in the business, that should be brought in order in the family.

To the woman: Now remember the feelings you just had towards this new business, and bring these feelings here, to this dead person. That's where they belong.

Hellinger leads her to the dead person again. She bends down to her and folds her hands.

HELLINGER *to the group:* I can interrupt it here. I have shown the central issue.

Further examples on this topic:

The order of rank:

FIRST EXAMPLE:
The priority of the employees 68

The inheritance:

FIRST EXAMPLE:
Questions of ownership .. 105

Sixth topic

The inheritance

Introductory remarks

Inheritance: A blessing and a curse

Goethe says about inheritance: "What you inherited from your fathers, earn it, in order to make it yours." In this sense an inheritance becomes a task.

The question is: Is this inheritance in accord with our personal destiny? Does it ease and further it? Does it serve it, can we serve our destiny together with our inheritance? Or does the inheritance put itself in the place of this destination and this calling? Does it become a burden for us or even a curse? Especially when the inheritance entangles us in something that takes us along into the consequences of some wrongdoing. For instance, if it was gained at the expense of others, perhaps even at the expense of their lives? How do we deal with such an inheritance?

To renounce it, would be the simple way, and it is often the right way.

A more demanding option would be, to accept the inheritance, but with the aim of carrying on with it in a good way. Then we pose to ourselves the task, to help something return to order that longs to be reconciled, with the help of the inheritance. Then we use and renounce it, both at the same time, both in the service of love.

Those expecting an inheritance, already making plans with it, are basically waiting for the death of the person they expect to inherit from. When they wait for their inheritance from their parents', what kind of relationship is left between them? What kind of a blessing for those who will receive it? Is it still worth anything? What is it worth?

Where several children inherit together, where there's a community of heirs, they often fight over their share. Especially where one child got a preferred treatment, or the opposite.

Where's the honoring of the parents gone? Where is their loving memory? Where's the gratitude, where's the love?

Such an inheritance is often squandered, against the parents intention. What else is squandered at the same time? How many gifts of life, that we received from our parents?

Such an inheritance easily turns into a curse. It takes something away, instead of giving it.

What especially in such an inheritance has the effect of diminishing life? It is gaining something without our own effort. As with money, when it came to us without effort and achievement on our part, so it is with an inheritance. It goes through our fingers like water, we cannot hold onto it.

Something else we observe about heirs, especially when it is a big inheritance. The bequeathed, how much is left for them of their lives? What are they still living for? What are the strange feathers worth that they decorate themselves with, compared to bread honestly earned, feeding us and our families?

It's a different matter if we dedicate the inheritance to the service of life. Then we gain it through an achievement. To the degree of our effort that we extend, we may own it. Then it becomes an expression of gratitude and love for those who passed it on to us. Especially for our parents when they leave us something, or for a partner who bequeathed us.

In the latter case there is something to keep in mind. Do the surviving partners remain free for another new partnership? Do they remain free for their own future? Which crown do they wear? Is it their own?

The basic rule is: No inheritance is earned. As soon as we acknowledge that, we become free of it. Especially, we become and remain free for our future. And we remain free from other people's envy. We only shine with our own light.

If there is a burden on the inheritance, we dispose of the burden by renouncing the inheritance. If there is a blessing on it, we take it as a blessing. We continue on, letting the inheritance act as a blessing, a rich blessing for many.

First example: *Questions of ownership*

From the course about the laws of successs in São Paulo • 31.3. – 1.4. 2009

Hellinger *to a young woman:* What is you issue?
Woman: I have a crisis in my business with my partners. It's about a business that belongs to four families: Three shareholders and a group of heirs.

Hellinger: Who owns the business?
Woman: My father is one of the partners who founded the business. He has one other partner in this business.

Hellinger: How did this partner join in?
Woman: They began together.

Hellinger: It belongs to both of them?
Woman: They founded it together. Then a third person joined, that was an heir. Then there was a fourth group of heirs, that also joined in. The third partner only came in twenty years later.
Hellinger *to the group:* Do you still get it?

All call out: No.

HELLINGER: Me neither.

To the woman: The heir inherited from whom?

WOMAN: From his own father.

HELLINGER: From your father?

WOMAN: There are four parts: my father, the second partner, who has been in the business from the beginning, the third who joined as an heir. It had belonged to his father, and then the third joined as an heir.

HELLINGER: Which father had owned that part?

WOMAN: It was like this. In the beginning there were two partners and two shareholders who only invested money. That makes it four at the beginning.

HELLINGER *to the group:* We have work to do there, in this confusion, where the legal positions of ownership are not clear. How can this business thrive?

So, something to keep in mind, a business is never owned by the shareholders. The shareholders bring money in the business. They can only acquire shares, not the business. A shareholder has no rights in a business, no permission to meddle. Shareholders bring money, but they have no rights to own a business. Can you follow me so far?

What is such a business, where the shareholders assume power, interested in? Does it focus on the product? Does it focus on the customers? Does it focus on the employees? It only looks at the money.

To the woman: What is your role in the business?

WOMAN: I don't work in the business. I represent my father who has Alzheimer's. He was the director of the business. He cannot work in the business any more, because the illness is already quite advanced

HELLINGER: Who is the director of the business now?

WOMAN: Today the leader is the one whom I called the heir of the shareholder.

HELLINGER: He is in charge of the business?

WOMAN: Yes, theoretically.

HELLINGER: And who practically? I wonder if one can get some order back into that?

WOMAN: The court intervened. My family asked for it, because they are denied access to the business.

HELLINGER: What shall the court decide?

WOMAN: In a business with 4 partners, there would have to be an election for the leadership, according to the law. But since my father is not in the business any more, there is a dispute about who should lead the business. My family and the other family are on one side, the other two partners on the other. They are not going away. The leadership would have to be newly elected, but they just don't leave their positions.

HELLINGER: Is the business insolvent?
WOMAN: No, there's profit, and it goes very well.

HELLINGER *to the group:* Let's begin to look for the order.

Hellinger chooses a representative for the business and places him. Then he chooses three representatives for the employees and three representatives for the customers and places them opposite the business, at a distance.

Then he chooses a representative for the product and a representative for the money. They stand in the middle between the business on one side and the customers and the employees on the other, with 3 meters in between them.

HELLINGER *to the group:* Now we'll watch what happens.

The business shakes all over its body. The product looks at the employees and the customers. Two employees are restless and shake their hands. One looks to the ground and lies down, still shaking heavily. Another employee goes nearer to the customers

After a while the product goes to the money and stands next to it. Both look to the customers. The business took some steps forwards, nearer to the customers. It is still shaking heavily. One of the customers goes to it and stands next to it. The employees remain at a distance. The product and the money withdraw a long way.

HELLINGER *to the woman:* Strange, that the business is shaking. Now I will get your father and the co- founder.

Hellinger chooses two men and places them side by side at some distance, with the business in view.

HELLINGER *to the woman:* The money and the product don't play a role any more, and the employees are not well. How many shareholders are there?
WOMAN: Four.

Hellinger chooses 4 representatives for the shareholders and asks them to find their own place. Two employees are still shaking heavily. The father goes closer to the business. The partner follows him, at some distance.

WOMAN: My father is a shareholder, the first partner also, then two more. In that regard we would only need two more shareholders.

HELLINGER: From the role here, I leave them as they are, as I chose them
WOMAN: Of the two shareholders . . .

HELLINGER: Let it be, this is only confusing. Is there a main customer?
WOMAN: Yes. The woman who stands next to the business.

The second partner has placed himself next to the business. The business reaches a hand out to him. Side by side, from left to right, all standing, is the second partner, the business, the main customer, and the father. The representatives of the additional shareholders stand further away. One of them embraces the product, another the money. A third one pushes in between the business and the second partner.

An employee is now standing in front of the business. Hellinger leads the second partner away.

HELLINGER *to the second partner:* How is it for you here?
SECOND PARTNER: *Better.*

HELLINGER: How is the business?
BUSINESS: Better now.
HELLINGER *to the main customer:* How are you?
CHIEF CUSTOMER: *I feel as if I were the support.*

HELLINGER: Well, you are the main customer.
To the representative of the employees who stands in front of the business: How are you?
THIS EMPLOYEE: I am very sad, because right from the beginning I wanted to be here, but my friends and colleagues are over there.

Hellinger: How is the money?
The Money: I hold on to the product and I ask the shareholder if he knows what to do now.

Hellinger *to a shareholder who stands a little apart:* What is with you?
This Shareholder: I feel as if I wanted to protect something or keep a place for someone.

Hellinger *to the shareholder who constantly strokes the product:* With you?
This Shareholder: I love the product. I look at the business, but I have no strength.

Hellinger takes the product to the employee who was lying on the ground shaking before. They embrace. A second employee joins them and also embraces the product. Slowly they move towards the business.

Hellinger *to the woman:* On whom does the product depend?
Woman: On the employees.

Hellinger: Exactly. Now you join them and find your place.

She stands to the left of her father, and takes the hand of the employee who stood in front of the business the whole time. Another employee who was shaking heavily before, stands behind her and puts his hands on her shoulders. The shareholder who pushed in between clings to the business.

Hellinger: How is the father now?
Father: I am better. I would love this employee (who was standing close to the business before) to be away from the main customer. I would like to create some distance between the two. It is as if she wanted to take something away from me.

This employee now stands in front of the main customer, with his back turned to her.

This Employee: My feeling towards her is very strong. I would like to be here, close to the father.
Hellinger *to the father:* How is that?
Father: *I become weaker.*

Hellinger places this employee with the other employees. Then he places the main customer with the other customers.

Hellinger *to the father:* How is it now?
Father: *Better.*

Hellinger: How is the business?
Business: *Worse.*

Hellinger takes the business to the main customer. Two of the employees go to the woman and the father again.

Business *to the main customer: You need me.*

Hellinger: How is the product now?
Product: *Better.*

The customers go to stand with the business. The business holds the main customer by the hand. An employee pulls the woman whose issue this is, along into this group. They all embrace.

Hellinger *to the woman:* This is the new business. Here it will continue. The product feels good, and the employee feels good, too.

Hellinger goes to the shareholders who are standing away from the others, together with the money, and asks them, how they are.

First Shareholder: Not very good.
The Money: Good.
Second Shareholder: Good.
Third Shareholder: Good.
Forth Shareholder: Somewhat difficult here.

Hellinger takes the shareholders way and the money separate from them.

HELLINGER *to the woman:* All of these are a burden. You know what this means? They get paid out. All of them. The business will come to life. Is it clear?
WOMAN: Yes. As clear as day.

HELLINGER *to the representatives:* Thank you all.
To the woman: The shareholders want to take something without contributing. They must be gone. The business is strong enough to master that. Okay so far?
WOMAN: Very good.

HELLINGER: After all this confusion we finally found a solution. The solution showed up through the movements we could observe. There was another power at work, full of goodwill for this business. You go with this movement – serving. All the best to you.
To the group: This was an example how to overcome the world economic crisis. Those who don't do anything shouldn't get anything either. Then everything resolves in a good way and serves life.

Questions

Hellinger: Any questions about that perhaps?

The wife's inheritance

A Woman: I would love to know, how it is with the order of things, when a woman gets an inheritance, but the husband decides what shall happen to it.

Hellinger: Well it will be lost.
Woman: That's what happens then?

Hellinger: Usually.
Woman *laughs: You have answered my question.*

Who owns a business?

Hellinger: Any more questions?
A Man: I would love to know, what the order is when a business is passed on. We know that many businesses are family businesses. What is the order, when fathers pass on the business to the children? This goes over many generations sometimes, that these business perpetuate themselves.

Hellinger: We would have to have a look at it. Do you have a special business in mind?
Man: I'm asking generally. I heard from a comment you made, that the heirs often don't deserve the inheritance.

Hellinger: That's true. A business does not belong to the owner. It doesn't belong to the children either. It belongs to those whom it serves. Therefore, a business is passed on to the one who is most willing to serve people. I lay myself open to attack here. A business must not be distributed amongst the so called heirs either.
Man: Can I ask something else about this?

Hellinger: Just a moment.
To the group: Can you understand what I mean? Can you feel it? This way, all are well. Those who, according to the law, would be entitled to a part of the inheritance, say: "We leave it there, where it serves best.". Then they can have something from the profit, of course. That is the same as always with a service, those who give something, also receive something. In this way they get back more that what they would have received if they had been paid out, because the business flourishes.

I have just said this like that. Just feel inside how it is for you. I'll give you a simple example.

Some people with a beautiful garden just have a small wooden fence around it. Many people walk past and enjoy the beautiful garden. Do the owners have less or more of this garden then?

Now when a high wall is built around it, do the owners have more of the garden or less ? Does the garden want to stay with them? Do things grow well in there? Or do the plants wilt in it? Just feel this inside. Everything we share with others so they can enjoy it as well, thrives.
To the Man: Thanks for the good question.

Resigning

A WOMAN: In this last constellation the founder resigned. How about the order here?

HELLINGER: He is severely ill. He resigns in the service of the enterprise. This has a good effect on the business.

SECOND EXAMPLE: *Inheritance: Yes or no?*

From the course in Curitiba, Brazil • 19. – 20. August 2008

HELLINGER: Anyone else here, who wants to make a decision?

A man puts his hand up and sits next to Hellinger .

HELLINGER: What is it about?

MAN: It's about an inventory, a family inventory. My parents separated 18 years ago. My father remarried later. So, he married again, with a total property settlement, also for the reason that a part of his inheritance came from his father in law, from his former wife's father.

So, when. . . – he talks and talks –

HELLINGER: Where there's so much talking, there's nothing that can be done anyhow.
To the Man: What exactly is it about? Who wants what here?
MAN: – talks again^ = ...

HELLINGER: Who wants what?
MAN: – talks again ^ = ...

HELLINGER: Who wants something, says it in one sentence! When people talk a lot, I don't need to know what they say. I know they're hiding something.
To the group: I'll say something about inheritance. No one deserves an inheritance! Those who look at the inheritance, are waiting for someone's death.
To the Man: Who are the people that are fighting?
MAN: Four children from the first marriage and one from the second.

HELLINGER: From whom does the inheritance come? Does it come from the father or the mother?

Man: How do you mean? I believe that the two of them built it up together.

Hellinger: Who bequeaths? Are you from the first marriage or from the second.
Man: From the first.
Hellinger *to the group:* There's a secret here. Perfectly clear. But I'll say something about inheritance.

A man marries and has a wife, and he has children with her. Then he marries a new woman. And he has children with here, too. Now it matters: How is the inheritance distributed?

Very often the second wife claims the inheritance, and and the children from the second relationship claim a share. This is very often the case. Then the children from the first marriage are often excluded

The consequences for the second wife and the children from the second marriage are terrible. They are terrible – I just point this out- and this over several generations.

I followed this up in the family of the famous German author Thomas Mann. A woman wrote a book about him and asked me to look at this family's history from the systemic perspective.

Many of the tragic things that happened in Thomas Mann's family derive from the fact that his grandfather did not give anything to his children from the first marriage. Instead, he gave everything to the children from the second marriage.

So here, the order of rank is essential. The first wife and the children from the first marriage come first. When the second wife misappropriates the inheritance, at the expense of the others, it has severe consequences.

The simplest thing is, not to inherit anything. Every inheritance brings a burden. Sometimes it also comes with a responsibility. For instance when someone takes on a business. This is a responsibility. Something is given to an heir, so that it will go on.

Very often, an inheritance is expected and accepted from a self-centered position, without giving the inheritance a task in the service of life. And that's what matters. When an inheritance is taken, in order to let it serve life, it is a precious inheritance.

I have also seen: Often, those who fight about an inheritance care more about the inheritance than about their children's life. Their whole concern centers around the inheritance, and they pay for the inheritance with their children's life.

So, freedom from inheritance is often the most beautiful option! What we earn ourselves, we have earned, and it stays. I'll leave it here.

... in law

Hellinger: We talk about parents in law, about the mother in law, the father in law, the son in law, the daughter in law. Certain feelings are connected to that, sometimes also certain expectations, or even claims. With the word ... in law connection are forged which, in my view, take something away from the essential relationship of parents to their children, and of children to their parents.

We just need to feel inside, which difference it makes when a man (concerning his wife's mother) speaks of my wife's mother, instead of his mother in law, or of his wife's father instead of his father in law. How does his wife feel? Reversely, how does the husband feel, when his wife also speaks about her husband's father or mother?

Stranger still, when a man speaks of this wife's children's partners from an earlier relationship, as his sons and daughters in law. Principally children only belong to their parents. Otherwise, what does he get involved in, where it is really none of his business?

It's a different matter when in a couple relationship the husband's or the wife's parents speak of their children's partners as their as their sons or daughters in law. For here something new is on the way. When their children become parents with their partners, they become grandparents.

But even here, from the feeling and the respect that goes with it, it would be more beautiful and serving the freedom of all involved more, when the children's father speaks of his wife's father as of the grandfather, rather than of his father in law, for as the grandfather he is now connected with the young family in a special way and a part of it. .

The same goes for his wife's mother, who has now also become his children's grandmother. Instead of mother in law the husband calls them more beautifully his children's grandmother.

Here, everything remains connected to what is essential, without giving rise to expectations and dependencies that rather burden than serve.

The words mother and father and son and daughter and grandmother and grandfather and granddaughter and grandson keep on shining brightly and full of clarity.

THIRD EXAMPLE: *Who bequeaths?*

From the course about the laws of success in São Paulo • 21.3. – 1.4. 2009

HELLINGER *to a woman:* What is it about?
WOMAN: I am entitled to an inheritance from my parents, and I intent to go to court about it.

HELLINGER: What kind of an inheritance is it?
WOMAN: It is the inheritance of a family business. The person who would have to pay me my share of the inheritance is my brother.

HELLINGER: So there is a family business? That was bequeathed to whom?
WOMAN: To my brother.

Hellinger: Who is the eldest child?
Woman: I am.

Hellinger: And it was bequeathed to him?
Woman: Yes.

Hellinger: What is the problem?
Woman: My father stated in his will, that our brother has to pay his sisters out. But he does not do it.

Hellinger: How many siblings are you?
Woman: Four, including me, four living children.

Hellinger: Where is your brother's place among the siblings?
Woman: He's the third child.

Hellinger: Is the second child a girl or a boy?
Woman: A girl.

Hellinger: The fourth child?
Woman: Is also a girl.
Hellinger *to the group:* Okay, the problem is clear.

Hellinger chooses a female representative for the inheritance, a representative for the brother, and three representatives for the sisters. He places them side by side in the order of age, opposite the inheritance, 5 meters away.

Hellinger *to the group:* Now we watch what happens.

Nobody moves.

Hellinger: I will place one more woman.

He chooses a representative for the mother and places her on a line with the inheritance, but four meters away from it.

The inheritance looks immediately at the mother. It turns to her and slowly moves closer to her.

The first and the second sister take each other by the hand and go closer to the mother. The brother stays firmly on his spot. The youngest sister takes a few steps forward, then turns around and looks back at the brother.

Hellinger *to the woman:* When we look at this: To whom does the inheritance belong?
Woman: To the mother.

Hellinger: Is she still alive?
Woman: No.

Hellinger: The inheritance is hers. It has to carry her name.

The woman goes to her mother. They embrace.

Hellinger to the brother who is still in his spot: How are you?

Brother: *Better.*

The second sister also goes the mother and embraces her together with the oldest sister.

Hellinger chooses a representative for the father. He places him slightly apart between the mother and the brother.

Hellinger to the brother: Tell you father: "I accept the inheritance from you for my mother."

He says it very loudly.

Hellinger: Say it with love.
Brother *to his father after much hesitation: I take the inheritance from you for my mother.*

The father's representative breathes deeply with relief. Hellinger takes him to stand in front of his mother.

Hellinger *to the father:* Tell her: "It's yours."
Father: *It is yours.*

Hellinger: "Yours alone."
Father: *Yours alone.*

Hellinger: Tell your son, too: "It's hers."
Father: *It's hers.*

Hellinger: "Hers alone."
Father: *Only hers.*

Hellinger: "I renounce it."
Father: *I renounce it.*

Hellinger: How is the inheritance?
Inheritance: *Very good now.*

The youngest sister stands to the right of their mother now and embraces her. The son goes slowly towards the mother.

Hellinger places the youngest sister in the position of the youngest. He places the son in the third place among the siblings, and the father to the right of the mother. As the father stands next to her, he puts his arm around her. Then, Hellinger places the inheritance opposite the mother.

Hellinger *to the woman:* Is it clear to you?
Woman: Yes.
Hellinger *to the representatives:* Thank you all.
To the group: Something else about inheritance. No one had earned it or deserves it. Who lets go of it is free. Who takes it must serve with it. Then the inheritance is in the service of life.

Seventh Topic

The double displacement

Introductory remarks

The Background

In a double displacement feelings are moved elsewhere. These are usually very painful feelings that cannot expressed out of a perceived powerlessness. They will be taken on by a later person or group, without them being aware of this displacement. They feel these feelings as if they were their own

This means: These feelings are looking for another carrier, another person who is not subject to an oppression that would make expressing these feelings a risky or outright dangerous matter, a person who could therefore express these feelings without inhibition. So it is a case of displacement of feelings from one subject onto another. This is the first part of the displacement

What makes this displacement twofold? These feelings are not just displaced in the subject, but also displaced concerning their object. This means, now a person or many people who did not suffer the painful treatment, are now directing the emotions to people or groups who were not involved in the original injustice, who are innocent as far as this injustice is concerned.

Just like the original people suffering the injustice were unable to defend themselves against the perpetrators in any way, those at whom these feelings are directed now, become defenseless victims.

It's time to give you an example. I take one from ordinary life, from a partner relationship.

A woman participated in a self-awareness group, together with her husband. The first evening she disappeared in their car. The next morning she arrives a little late for the group session, stands in front of her husband and tells him: "I'm just coming from my boyfriend."

The woman was friendly and caring towards the people in the group. But towards her husband, she often went completely berserk, even though her husband let her carry on without any attempt of defense. The others in the group did not understand what she was on about.

Later the background for her behavior came to light.

When she was a child, during the summer holidays her father sent the mother and the children to a place in the country, whilst he stayed in the city with his girlfriend. Occasionally he visited his wife and children together with this girlfriend. His wife waited upon both if them in a friendly way.

Such a behavior used to be called a heroic virtue in the olden days. But what happened to this woman's feelings, in her soul and in her heart? What helpless rage must she have felt that she did not dare express?

This suppressed rage was later taken on by her daughter, by this woman in the workshop. This was the first displacement. However the woman did not direct this rage at her father, for against him, she was also powerless. She directed it against her puzzled, non aggressive man. This was the second displacement.

At the same time she became similar to her father. She also had a relationship with another man, and she demonstrated it in front of her husband with no concern for his feelings.

Does this double displacement also play an role in business and organizations? Apparently yes. In some campaigns for instance, in some human rights organizations, in some peace demonstrations, in certain ideologically tainted institutions. It is also widespread, for instance in relationship between women and men, as a reaction against what many men did to women in the past. The suppressed rage of the women from earlier generations is later felt by the female descendents of these women, towards their men. What far reaching consequences this can have in the present time, is made clear to us in the following example.

Example: Double displacement in women and men in China

From the course about the laws of success in business in Hong Kong ◂ 14. – 16. June 2009

Hellinger *to a woman:* What kind of an enterprise is your issue about?
Woman: It's about a teaching enterprise. It has been in existence for twelve years.

Hellinger: Is this enterprise yours?
Woman: Yes, I founded it.

Hellinger: How many children are taught there?
Woman: I don't know.

Hellinger: How many employees do you have?
Woman: Two hundred.

Hellinger: No wonder you don't know the exact number of students. What is your issue here?
Woman: I would love to bring certain insights about education to the attention of a larger public. I would like to find out what

future my enterprise has, and how the relationships to the larger public can be improved.

Hellinger: On whom does the future of this school depend?
Woman: On other people.

Hellinger: On which people?
Woman: On people who have some understanding of life.

Hellinger: The future of the school depends above all on the parents of the children. Are they included? Are they fully included?
Woman: The future depends on the mothers.

Hellinger: Above all, you must gain the support of the fathers.
As she wants to respond: Wait.
To the group: I have brought something hidden to light. We saw it in her reaction. She wants to exclude the fathers.
To this woman: Where does the future lie?
Woman: I don't know.

Hellinger: Of course you know, everybody knows. The future of your enterprise depends on the fathers of these children.
To the group: Shall we have a closer look at this?

Broad consent from the audience

Hellinger: I do something really simple.

Hellinger chooses a woman for the future and gets her to stand somewhere. Opposite her he places a representative for the fathers. Then he chooses a woman as a representative for the mothers and gets her to stand to the left of the representative for the men. The future looks only at the fathers.

Hellinger *to the woman:* Where does the future look?

After a while as the future gets restless: We have seen it clearly.
To the representatives: Thank you all.

Loud applause from the audience

Hellinger *to the woman:* That was a surprise for you. As you have already done a lot of good work, you'll also be successful in this. So how would you proceed here, to be successful? I talk like a teacher now.

The woman smiles and agrees.

Hellinger: You guide the mothers in a way that they respect their husbands. This is not an easy task.
To the group: I will demonstrate it here.

Hellinger chooses a woman and asks her to stand as a representative. Then he chooses ten women and gets them to stand behind the first woman, very close together.

Hellinger *as the woman laughs, to the group:* Now it's getting serious.
To these representatives: The women behind you represent Chinese women from the past, who had to suffer a lot from their men. Turn to them.

After a while: Say to them: "I see you."

Representative: *I see you.*

Hellinger: "You have a place in my heart."
Representative *in tears: You have a place in my heart.*

The representative can hardly stand on her feet.

Hellinger after a while: Say to them: "Please help me to look at men differently."
Representative: Please help me to look at men differently.

Hellinger: So that they also learn to look at women differently.
Say: I'll take you along into another future.
Representative: *"I'll take you along into another future.*

Hellinger: For women and men together.

Representative: *For women and men together.*

Hellinger: Now turn around and feel how they stand behind you.

Hellinger turns her around. Then he places three men, side by side, in front of her.

Hellinger *to this representative:* Look at them.
Representative: *They look beautiful.*
Hellinger: That's the first discovery for you.

Hellinger asks the woman who is the school director, to stand next to this representative.

She takes this representative's hand and goes to the men with her. They all embrace. Then the school director herself withdraws.

Hellinger chooses two representatives for her school's students. She takes these by the hand and also leads them to the men. All embrace warmly. The school director herself remains at a distance.

Hellinger takes them to the women who represent the suppressed Chinese women from the past. She looks at them and weeps bitterly. Then she takes two of them and brings them to the men. They embrace. The women sob loudly. They turn to the other women. They reach their hands out to them so that they might also come closer.

As these hesitate, the school director takes one man by the hand to bring him to the women who stayed behind. As she notices that one

of these women sobs loudly, she takes this woman by the hand, to take her to the men. Then this woman breaks down sobbing loudly, and she turns to the women who are still staying away.
The school director is now standing with her back to the women who remained behind, as if she wanted to protect them from the men.

One of the women who stands in the group with the men, calls out to her: "Pluck up your courage. Come back, otherwise we have no chance. The children also belong to the men. Pluck up your courage. Give yourself a chance. We belong together."

Some of the women who stayed behind would rather stay behind than go to the men. The school director wants to take them by the hand, but they refuse. The other woman calls out to her: "Come back. Leave the others to their fate. You belong here with us."

HELLINGER *after a while:* I leave it here.
To the representatives: Thank you all.
To the school director as she sits next to him again: Do you know what happened here? A cultural revolution. Now you know where your school's future lies. All the best to you.

Loud applause from the group

Explanations

Hellinger *to the group:* I owe you an explanation about the background that came to light in this constellation. World wide, not just in China, many women had to suffer much contempt and suppression and violence from men. Their fate is still having many effects in the present time though the people involved, especially the women, may not be aware of it. All of this has far reaching consequences for the relationship between women and men, men and women, be it in the couple relationship, be it as parents, and also in business and other larger associations. And we have to acknowledge that men still discriminate against women, putting them down and rejecting them in many different ways. So many women still have good reason to feel put down.

In spite of the changes in out time the fate of the suppressed women from the past still exerts its effects in a largely subconscious manner, affecting couple relationships even now.

What is my observation in this? Years ago I discovered, that in many relationships the dynamics of a double displacement are still operating. What does this mean, concerning women?

Many women feel a deep connection in their soul with the fate of the women in their family, from the time where patriarchy dominated. They see the feelings these women carried, feelings of suppressed rage, of pain, of the absence of hope to be able to change their fate. Secretly they take these feelings over from them, even if they realize, they live in a different situation and have much better options to better their lives, so that they have less or no reason to have those feelings on a personal level. This means: the suppressed feelings of women from former times are taken on by their descendents, without these becoming aware of it. This would be the first displacement, the displacement of feelings that other women had before them, onto their descendents, without these having a similar reason for them. So far so good.

This taking on of feelings by women of later generations becomes tragic through the fact that these feelings want to be expressed. They cannot be expressed towards those who were responsible for them, since they have long died. And on a deeper level, even in the female descendents an inability to relate to these ancestor men might still be at work. In every regard, the angry and desperate feelings are expressed in a safe way by women in the present towards men in the present. They may just take the appearance of a certain distance, but often there are also loud and clear and hostile expressions towards their husbands, even though these do not give any comparable reason for it. This is the second displacement. The feelings from the past are displaced on men in the present – again, largely unconsciously so.

The question is: What chance do such men have in their relationship with their wives? Are they seen by them, as they are? Or do they see in them other men, who have nothing in common, nothing to do, with their husbands?

We have seen here how such a double displacement can be brought to light and resolved, in the service of love for all.

At the same time we have seen that the double displacement can also be at work in a business, to the detriment of many. Where a business has no future, a double displacement can be one of the causes.

Now imagine, which future can be in store for many couple relationships and what happiness for many children- and the same goes for businesses when these deep causes are taken into account. Imagine women being allowed to take on places equal to men, and imagine women recognizing that many men are willing to acknowledge women as equals, and at the same time both genders seeing and respecting their being different.

Sexuality and death

From the intensive camp
in Barcelona • 4. – 11. September 2009

Hellinger: Sexuality is an event against death. What does sexuality acknowledge above all? Death. What does sexuality want to overcome? Death.

Sexuality is closely connected to death. It costs the most lives. Those who can survive many dead can live.

There is also a strange image. Who looks primarily at life? Who leads more into life? Man woman, or woman man? Man, very definitely. Man stands for life primarily. Who saves a child from death? Man above all.

Another strange observation: Women are closer to death. I don't know if I'm allowed to say all that. These are images that come. You can check it inside yourselves, what the inner movement is. I'll say it to the extreme. The woman looks rather at the death of the child than at its life. Therefore the children are more secure with their fathers than with their mothers.

This one is a superficial observation. The life of a woman is more in danger than the life of a man, in many regards, through the life that gets lost through sexuality for instance, through miscarriage or abortion. A woman is quite differently connected with the life that is lost than a man. So, through the losses that cost life, the woman is more connected to death than to life.

Can you feel that ? This is the movement in her. This is something basic. I don't have the time now to enlarge on that. But I could come back to it when we have questions and answers tonight. Agreed?

Agreeing in the group

Continuation: Life at the expense of death

I would like to say something else about death. Sexuality has a function in the face of death. It is an endeavor against death.

Why do people want to have children? Why must they have children? Because they die. The children will make sure later that they stay alive. In earlier days, those who had no children were lost. On the one hand, the children safeguarded their survival, on the other hand they lived on in their children.

But the children's life and the parents' survival comes often at the expense of the death of other family members. Especially for the woman, passing life on is closely connected with danger to life, with personal danger for her life. She is also connected with death because some of the life she carries inside, dies. For instance when a child dies prematurely, in the womb, or when the mother wants the child to die, often with the idea that she can live better then. She sacrifices a child for her own survival. Life and death are close together here, especially for the woman.

Inner movements away from life, towards death

There is a domain of authority in us, that also leads to death. This authority is our conscience.

When a woman loses a child or kills it, she is also drawn into the death of the child. She feels an inner longing to follow the child.

Another idea plays a role here. As a man I must not claim to know much and to say much. I cannot feel women's feelings the same way as a woman. I refer mostly to what I see in constellations, but also what my wife Sophie explained to me in many ways.

There is an idea that appears to play a role here. In an abortion a woman loses a part of her body. This is an image in some women. Then they try to reclaim what is lost in a number of ways, for instance – his is my image – through certain gynecological problems. It appears that myomas also represent something that was lost.

So, in many ways the woman is drawn into movements that lead to death. At least, the idea is there: It draws me into death.

But you need not despair. That is the initial situation. The question is: Is there another way?

First of all, back once more to conscience. In much of what happens to women, conscience plays a role. For instance in many ways, when she blames herself. This feeling of guilt she wants to get rid of then, so to speak. From this feeling there is an inner movement to become like the child, when a child died or was miscarried or aborted. This is meant to ease the guilt feelings, – but at the price of life. So, all these movements that result from guilt or from penance for guilt are movements towards death.

Can you follow me in this? So, all this opposes life, it also opposes the goal of sexuality.

Sexuality that creates and brings forth life and thus serves life, turns into its opposite in this movement. The result is that sexuality ceases or is rejected, that sexuality is no longer taken along into the movement of life.

There are many other causes and situations. For instance when a woman withdraws from her husband, because she holds him responsible one way or another for what brings her closer to death.

Movements of life

Now, we are all caught in conscience, we are in the thrall of conscience. In many constellations we can see that. Now it matters for us to find the strength, a force of life, that overcomes death. A force that bypasses the movements leading to death in a variety of ways, so that we can free ourselves from the movements to death.

The essential thing is that we let the dead people be dead, all the dead ones, whose death we connect with sexuality. This means the children who were not born, for whatever reasons, even if the mother and here also the father feel responsible for the child's death.

One thing needs to be perfectly clear. Life costs life. Life goes on because other life dies. What we eat has died. We live through the death of other life. This is a law of life. Much has to die so that some life can be maintained.

Can you still listen? Shall I go on?

Consenting from the group

Well I tell you, what I am saying now, I have never said before in this way. I trust my inner guidance and follow it, and I know I am moving within certain boundaries.

The problems we come across in this work here, are all connected to the fact that someone wants to join the dead. I'll say it quite extremely now: We don't acknowledge, that these dead who were sacrificed for the lives of others, so that those lives can continue, want the others to live. Their death serves life. So, in accord with the dead, the movement in accord with them would be a movement that allows them be dead, that acknowledges their death.

But usually we can't do that – because of the guilt feelings. This need not involve personal guilt, it is enough for us to perceive: we gain something through their death. For this advantage we want to pay. With what? With death. The law of balance plays a role here.

How can we overcome this vortex into death? Family constellations in the form of going with a movement of the spirit show us a way. I will walk it with you now, in a meditation, so you can experience it inside yourselves. Just close your eyes, then we can do it inside.

Meditation: The decisive step

We feel in our body and in our emotions how we are drawn to some dead persons. We sense how in our thoughts and in our feelings many dead take hold of us. We sense the pull with which they draw us to themselves, into death.

In this, we also sense another movement. These dead want to live in us, instead of being dead. They themselves did not succeed in a movement towards their own death, and we cannot free ourselves from them of our own accord.

Now comes the decisive step. We look ahead. We think only of what is before us, we live only forwards. We slip out of our own skin as it were, out of our old skin of the dead, and we move forward – forward and into the wide open. We move into another depth, further and further, taken along by a creative movement of life, towards more life, more health, more joy, more fulfilled love – together.

And the dead we leave behind now, what are they doing? They finally close their eyes – all of them.

Postscript

How do I become and remain a good entrepreneur?

First: By having something to offer that serves others. The more they need it, the more important is what I can offer. In that case there is no further obstacle to my success.

What qualities define entrepreneurs? They have what others need, and they make it available to them. The more they have of what others need, the higher their prestige and their success.

Conclusion: Entrepreneurs serve. The more important their service, the greater their influence.

Second: Entrepreneurs need helpers. They must attract employees and educate and train them, so that what the enterprise offers is produced, marketed, and sold the best way.

So, what they have to offer, they must produce and also sell.

Third: Entrepreneurs must lead. They lead through their ideas. They lead through the production. They lead through selling and everything that goes with it.

Fourth: Entrepreneurs face competition. Through competition they improve their product. Through this, those who need it, are served all the better.

Fifth: Entrepreneurs defend their enterprises against encroachment and safeguard them accordingly. They remain self assured and self reliant.

Sixth: Entrepreneurs know that they depend on others with whom they have to cooperate. They know how to gain and to keep these others.

Seventh: Entrepreneurs love their success, it makes them happy. When an entrepreneur is happy and shows it, the employees and their families are also happy.

Eighth: Entrepreneurs form a community of solidarity with many. They know the happiness of many depend on their success. Hence they increase it with the help of many who help them to safeguard the livelihood of many.

Ninth: Entrepreneurs find the right time to hand their enterprise over to suitable successors. They leave them room to move, which they need to be successful. Yet they continue to remain their enterprise's soul. Their benevolent spirit lives on in the enterprise.

Tenth: Entrepreneurs go along with the development, that the enterprise must take, even if this is not in line with their ideas. They leave their enterprise to the river of time that eventually overtakes them, and they follow their journey with thoughts of good will.

References to further Book from the series: Orders of Success

Success in Life,
Success in Business
How they succeed together
108 pages. 1. Edition 2009
ISBN 978-3-00-029157-9
Hellinger Publications

This long-awaited book offers an uncommon perspective on one of the most common questions that people have: how to attain and maintain success in our work life. Familiar to many are the books comprised of techniques and tools designed for achieving this goal. And equally familiar to many is the corresponding disappointment when these techniques and tools are not effective in the long run.

At the heart of Bert Hellinger 's perspective is the understanding that the problem is not in the strategies themselves but in a fundamental disconnection between how we approach life and how we approach work. The two cannot be separated.

Succinct and profound, this book bridges the gap, explaining how rejection in one area is often translated into rejection in the other.

Perhaps ...

... an interruption in the movement to the mother has led to recurrent self-sabotage in the workplace,

... old models of masters and slaves are still influencing the current dynamics of an organization,

... the entrepreneur cannot follow through because her underlying attention is with the dead,

... a product or vision is out of alignment with the good of the people for whom it is meant,

... judgment steeped in generational prejudices are fragmenting the work team.

More generally, perhaps current work-related quests often meet unseen resistance that is actually located in the unreconciled scenarios of the past rather than in the details of the present. The discussion here is about the deep principles of success in all spheres of life. Once this type of backdrop is in place, achieving success is no longer in the chase but in being in tune with what actually wants to happen when we are prepared.

Stories of Success in Business and Profession

Paperback, 244 pages
1. Edition 2009
ISBN 978 -3-00-029328-3
Hellinger Publications

This book draws from life's fullness. It stays close to the pulse of life and tells stories: gripping stories, where we hold our breath at times, and stories of relief, where we experience with the people involved, how the decisive steps were taken successfully. Sometimes it also tells tragic stories, where failure is looming on the horizon and appears inevitable. However, even these stories show how something can begin anew, differently, in the service of life, in the service of our lives and in the service of many others.

Biographie

About Bert Hellinger

Bert Hellinger, a former priest and missionary to the Zulu in South Africa for 16 years, as well as an educator, psychoanalyst, group dynamic expert and family therapist, he brings vast and diverse experience to his work. Helping professionals everywhere have embraced the new possibilities that this innovative approach offers to their work. The family constellations, which have become the hallmark of Hellinger's approach, as well as his observations about – and insights into – family entanglements and their resolution, have touched the lives of thousands throughout the world.

Bert Hellinger has written more than 50 books, many of them available in other languages, 22 languages so far, including Arabic, Mongolian and Chinese. He is a philosopher in his own right and a teacher of wisdom as his late books testify.

Addresses

Online Shop

www.hellinger-shop.com

Homepage

www.hellinger.com

Email:

info@hellingerschule.com